T0114904

Prayer
OF
DESPERATION

The Seven {WE} of Spiritual Growth

Taken from 2 Chronicles 20:7 (KJV)

*Art thou not our God, who didst drive out the inhabitants
of this land before thy people Israel, and gavest it
to the seed of Abraham thy friend for ever?*

By: Evangelist Jerry Quinn

WESTBOW
PRESS®
A DIVISION OF THOMAS NELSON
& ZONDERVAN

WestBow Press books may be ordered through booksellers or by contacting:

WestBow Press
A Division of Thomas Nelson & Zondervan
1663 Liberty Drive
Bloomington, IN 47403
www.westbowpress.com
844-714-3454

Scripture quotations are taken from the Holy Bible, King James Version.

ISBN: 979-8-3850-1379-1 (sc)
ISBN: 979-8-3850-1380-7 (e)

Library of Congress Control Number: 2023923128

Print information available on the last page.

WestBow Press rev. date: 11/29/2023

I wrote *Prayer of Desperation* for the sole purpose of higher learning. It is an open-forum study guide for individual or group study with power scriptures for meditation. *Prayer of Desperation* has questions at the end of the book to answer. All scripture in this book is at the back of the book for your study.

All scripture is from the King James Version (KJV). All comments and definitions are my own. Some definitions have been included from Webster's Dictionary.

CONTENTS

WORDS OF POWER AND KNOWLEDGE

My greatest intention is to bring us into another depth of our spiritual walk with God, for to grow in grace is to grow in knowledge. From the beginning of time, God wanted his people not to be ignorant to his word, but to understand his word.

To stand on your own in the Lord is to be strong in the Lord, for faith is yours and yours alone. You have gained it, and you have grown with it. No one except you can take it away.

The whole source of your daily walk is to be ready for any joy and trials that will come. It is the lifeline of our growth. Understanding what it takes to grow and how we are to grow is the first step to growth. This catalyst carries us into the next area of God's blessing. To understand that is to understand we are the vessel of strength with all power given unto us. Now read and learn and be the best in God and the best for God. Amen.

POWER SCRIPTURES
FOR MEDITATION

These are power scriptures for meditation. They will build your confidence and faith in yourself and God. Learn them, meditate on them, and quote them every day, all day, and see yourself grow in the Lord.

- **John 14:14:** If ye will ask any thing in my name, I will do it.

  If we ask anything in his name and believe, it is ours. Now start exercising your privileges.

- **Job 22:28:** Thou shall also decree a thing, and it shall be established unto thee: and the light shall shine upon thy ways).

  If you speak over a thing and call or decree it, it will have to obey; to decree a thing is to take charge over a thing. In other words, take charge.

- **Romans 5:17:** and calleth those things which be not as thou they were.

  Whatsoever you call into existence will come to pass if you believe, but don't ask amidst.

- **Mark 11:23:** For verily I say unto you, that whosoever shall say unto this mountain, be thou removed, and be thou cast into the sea; and shall not doubt in his heart but shall believe that those things which he saith shall come to pass, he shall have whatsoever he saith.

  We must speak to the mountain and tell it what to do. God then says where to go and then believe, if we believe it is ours.

- **Matthew 16:19:** And I will give unto you the keys of the kingdom of heaven: and whatsoever thou shalt bind on earth shall be bound in heaven: and whatsoever thou shalt loose on earth shalt be loosed in heaven.

  We are to bind or lose what we want or what we want to get rid of. The authority is in our words, so speak to them.

- **Matthew 7:7:** Ask, and it shall be given you; seek and ye shall find; Knock, and it shall be open unto you.

  If we ask it in his name and believe, it is ours.

- **Isaiah 54:17:** No weapon that is formed against thee shall prosper.

  We are not to worry because no weapon formed against us can prosper. In other words, it might come, but we will fight back with the word and stand firm.

INTRODUCTION

This study manual covers how to overcome things in life. It goes over a lot of ground, addressing various subjects from faith to self-discipline, the power of positive thinking and positive speech, sanctification, believing and receiving, what to do when in desperation, how to pray under certain situations, and the call of leadership. This book intends to bring us to a place where we can draw nearer to one another and help us enter a deeper relationship with the Lord Jesus Christ.

I have included passages for scripture learning and memorization, along with many questions to answer. A quiz at the end of the book will allow you to examine yourself. If you study this book in an open forum, such as a classroom, it will take about ten weeks to complete, if you study one night a week. I recommend you read the whole book first and then have a group to study with.

Now this book is taken from 2 Chronicles 20:1–4.

> It came to pass after this also, that the children of Moab, and the children of Ammon, and with them other besides the Ammonites, came against Jehoshaphat to battle. Then there came some that told Jehoshaphat, saying. There cometh a great multitude against thee from beyond the sea on the side Syria, and behold, they be in Hazazontamar, which is Engedi. And Jehoshaphat feared, and set himself to seek the Lord, and proclaimed a fast throughout all Judah. And Judah gathered themselves together, to ask of the Lord: even out of all the cities of Judah came to seek the Lord.

What a coming together the children of Israel did when faced with a situation. That is what it's all about, my friend, the coming together in faith and unity to bring about victory and joy.

How can you tell me how to be saved if you are not? You can't! The word of God shares many fascinating things and includes many great stories that tell the rise and fall of mankind and the deliverance of mankind for our learning.

In this story of Jehoshaphat, we will learn what to do when faced with certain life situations. Jehoshaphat's story is very entreating and full of great knowledge and instruction. It is for our receiving, if we will.

As we journey through this subject, I hope you will grow in faith, power, understanding of the word, and fullness of your God-called ministry. May God bless you in your study!

Before you go any further, ask yourself, *Do I want to grow in grace?*

What did Jehoshaphat do when he got word of the army encamped around them? List three things.

SUBJECTS OF GREAT TRUTH

Look at what it is to receive. It is great when we learn how to receive and learn what we have been given to us just for being a child of God. The woman at the well did not understand what he said but took him at his word because she went to the city and began to tell everybody in John 4:29, "Come see a man, which told me all things ever I did."

As you can see what it did to her, it can do to you as well. She received the word and went forth, telling the good news. She received. Now will you?

If I ask, "How is your car?" you will automatically see your car. Why? A word was spoken to reveal your car. So is the word of God. If I say you can have whatsoever you ask in his name, you automatically start thinking about things you need. Why again? The word is a seed that opens up the ground to be planted. Romans 10:17 reads, "Faith cometh by hearing and hearing by the word of God."

Also recognize that it stands true for bad words. Let someone say anything about something that has happened to you, like the death of a child, someone lying on you, adultery in the family, or abuse. What happens to you? You see it as it was because the ground was open and a seed was planted.

Now we can do one of two things. We can rebuke it and let the ground shut before the seed takes root, but sometimes in my life, the root has taken root so quickly that I could not believe it. I was upset, mad, and depressed all in one second. But to receive the good words, we must let the seed plant and flourish so it brings life.

> Art thou greater than our father Jacob, which gave us the well, and drank thereof himself, and his children, and his cattle? Jesus answered and said unto her, whosoever drinketh of this water shall thirst again: But whosoever drinketh of the water that I shall give him shall never thirst; but the water that I shall give him shall be in him a well of water springing up into everlasting life. The woman saith unto him, Sir, give me this water, that I thirst not, neither come hither to draw. Jesus saith unto her, Go, call thy husband, and come hither. The woman answered and said, I have no husband. Jesus said unto her, thou hast well said, I have no husband: For thou hast had five husbands; and he whom thou now hast is not thy husband: in that saidst thou truly. The woman saith unto him, Sir, I perceive that thou art a prophet. Our fathers worshipped in this mountain; and ye say, that in Jerusalem is the place where men ought to worship. Jesus saith unto her, Woman, believe me, the hour cometh, when ye shall neither in this mountain, nor yet at Jerusalem, worship the Father. Ye worship ye know not what: we know what we worship: for salvation is of the Jews. But the hour cometh, and now is, when the true worshippers shall worship the Father in spirit and in truth: for the Father seeketh such to worship him. God *is* a Spirit: and they that worship him must worship *him* in spirit and in truth. The woman saith unto him, I know that Messias cometh, which is called Christ: when

he is come, he will tell us all things. Jesus saith unto her, I that speak unto thee am *he*. And upon this came his disciples, and marvelled that he talked with the woman: yet no man said, What seekest thou? or, why talkest thou with her? The woman then left her waterpot, and went her way into the city, and saith to the men, she took him at his word and went forth to tell all she heard and knew. (John 4:12–29)

Only God can give us peace over some things, so we must hear the word and determine which voice is speaking. Only when we can hear what the spirit says can we really see what is being said. The spirit builds up and restores you to your full potential. By the goodness of the Lord, we are able to overcome our battles.

When we become what the word says, we will become a spiritual house. Use by the Lord and for the Lord to bring forth victory to others and ourselves. It is all by receiving the word, my brother and sister.

I have spent many years trying to get people to understand that, as people, we are living way below our means. There are promises upon promises in the word of God just waiting for our receiving. But do we want them enough to receive them?

Now let's wait a minute here! To receive from God, we must first be a willing vessel and a receiving vessel with a clean heart. When we become willing to partake of the fruits of his blessing and goodness, we are to give blessing and goodness back to the Father. The woman at the well gave the Lord all of her attention, and you can see what happened. What Jesus was saying electrified her, and she left and went about telling all. Why? She heard the word, received the word, and spoke about the words she had heard. She went about telling all things she had heard and seen.

That doesn't mean we will not have any problems because we will. But I believe this book will help you understand our privileges and how we can apply our problems to the word of God.

We must comprehend the word of God because of its strength, power, faith, healing, joy, comfort, and much, much more. Time and room will not let me write all of what the word is to me, but he is everything. As a child of God, we need to know what he said we can have and then learn how to receive it in the scripture and apply it to our needs.

We have taken a back seat to the word of God, and now we are powerless and vulnerable to everything the devil has to throw at us. The devil has stolen our freedom, children, and finances, and we are at the point where he has stolen our nation. We are so far behind in what should be ours that the world has taken control over us instead of us having control over the world.

God has called us to take back what is rightfully ours and do it now. You may ask, "What is ours?" The answer is this: our healing, our victory, our children, our finances, our home, our city, our country, our worship, and our freedom.

List the keys to our success and where Satan has robbed us.

As children of God, we need to do a lot of work. If we don't take back the nine things listed above, we, as a Christian nation, will be lost, and the freedom we share will vanish.

I know this is dropping a lot in your lap now, but I feel it is needed. We are living in critical times, and I don't feel I can express it enough. If we don't get a grip on what is happening around us and act now and take charge of the situation, our children will grow up not knowing the real blessing of God. Judges 2:10 says, "There rose another generation after them, which new not the Lord, nor yet the works which he had done for Israel."

This is what I am talking about. I'm so afraid that we have gotten so far from the signs, wonders, and miracles that this generation doesn't even know what it is to see the power of God move in the midst of them.

When Moses read the Book of Law to the children of Israel in Deuteronomy 28, he was teaching them what God expected from them and what they could expect from God. I encourage you to read the entire chapter of Deuteronomy 28 to get a better understanding of his promises. These were promises given to them, and they are also given to us. ("And there's no respecter of person," reads Colossians 3:25.)

In the book of Deuteronomy, God promises us some things that, if we will walk in his statutes and keep his commandments, these promises will be applied to us in this hour as it was applied to them when Moses read it.

Read a passage from both Deuteronomy 29:2–6 and Deuteronomy 28:12–13 so you can see all the wonderful promises that God has pronounced to us.

> And all these blessing shall come on thee, and overtake thee, if thou shall hearken unto the voice of the Lord thy God. Blessed shall be the fruit of thy body, and the fruit of thy ground, and the fruit of thy cattle, the increase of thy kine, and the flock of thy sheep, Blessed shalt thou be when thou goest out. Blessed shall be thy basket and thy store. Blessed shalt thou be when thou comest in and blessed shalt thou be when thou goest out. The Lord shall cause thine enemies that rise up against thee to be smitten before thy face; they shall come out against thee one way and flee before thee seven ways. (Deuteronomy 29:2–6)

> and thou lend too many nation, and thou shall not borrow. And the Lord shall make thee the head, and not the tail; and thou shall be above and not beneath. (Deuteronomy 28:12–13)

We are somebody to never to be beneath, to be the tail, or to be in debt, which a lot of us are. We shall be blessed in the fruit of our ground, fruit of our body, and fruit of our cattle and the increase of thy kine, and when thou comest in and when thou comest out, thy store and thy basket shall be full. (There are seven promises here mentioned.)

The provisions are there. We just need to learn how to apply them to our situation and never be under the enemy's feet again. We have the provisions, so let's take charge of our situation now and line up with the word of God and receive our blessing.

I want to talk about seven things called the "Seven We of Growth to Prosperity," and I believe, if we take them to heart, the blessing of God will multiply in our life. The word *prosperity* here is not only talking about riches of money, even though I believe the Lord wants us to prosper in finances. But John said in 3 John 2, "Beloved, I wish above all things that thou mayest prosper and be in health, even as thy soul prospereth."

There is a lot more to prospering than just being rich in money, even though I know we must have it to live in these societies. Being rich in God's blessing is the most important thing we could ever want. To have favor with him, to know we have his blessing upon us, and to meet our every need is a great consolation and worthy to be praised and receive.

Explain why the Seven We of Growth to Prosperity is so important.

THE SEVEN WE OF GROWTH TO PROSPERITY

1. We have to take back what is ours by acting on the word.
2. We have to learn who we are in the Lord and what our privileges are in the Lord.
3. We have to know that our faith in the name of Jesus moves mountains.
4. We have to realize the need for a move of God's spirit.
5. We have to realize that God's word is the only thing that can tear down walls when applied.
6. We have to hold to the altar of salvation for the unbeliever and oneself.
7. We must not ever back down from the devil … never.

These seven statements are the spiritual growth we, as Christians, are lacking. We read the word and pray, but we fail to do these seven. And because of it, we are lacking in a lot of areas.

We are somebody in Christ Jesus. Now how do we achieve all this? Well, here is a start! I believe in the power of positive speaking.

My wife was cooking supper, and she had gotten on the subject of our situation and how bad it was, talking like there was no way we were coming out of this mess we were in, how nothing seemed to be working, and how we were going backward.

The Lord spoke to me and told me to take her hand. So I got up, went over to her at the stove, and asked her to let me see her hand.

She asked, "Why?"

I said, "Just let me hold your hand."

She asked, "What are you going to do?"

I said, "Just let me see your hand."

And she reached out really slow, and I grabbed her hand and spoke, "We are going to agree that if you will not say another word concerning our situation for ninety days and if God does not turn it around, well, after the ninety days, I will never say anything to you about how you talk about our situation. Do you agree?"

She said, "Yes."

It was not easy for her, and occasionally she'd start speaking about how bad it was. I would just say, "Do you remember the agreement we made together? You need to watch what you are saying."

Within two months, God turned it around for us, and I heard nothing concerning how bad our situation was again. The Lord used my wife to show both of us a great truth during trying times.

Now the situation arrived about five years later while riding to Rockingham, North Carolina, to see a person. We were going through another hard time, but this time, the Lord gave us some very important words, which I hold to this day.

On our way there, we talked about different things we thought the Lord wanted us to do and some things we wanted to do for him. While we were talking about what we thought the Lord was showing us at that time, we were in complete agreement. Nothing could separate us, I thought.

As we were riding a little further, she began to change her mind and started talking like nothing would ever happen.

I asked, "What is this? A while ago, we both were in total compliance to what we believed God would do for us, but now it's changed."

About that time, the Lord spoke to me. "You tell her I said, 'Look, the Lord said for me to tell you, 'Look not for a reason why it won't work, but look for every reason why it will work.'"

She got really quiet, and I asked, "Did you hear that?"

She said, "Yes."

"Well, now look at all you see wrong and everything that is against us, and now look how it can work, even though it looks hopeless. And if you keep looking, you will see a light somewhere in the midst of the storm, and hope will come alive again, but you have to look for it. Sometimes it is hidden from us so we can't see it very well, but we have to hunt for it because it is always there."

1 Corinthians reads, "There hath no temptation taken you but such is common to man: but God is faithful, who will not suffer you to be temped above that ye are able ; but will with the temptation also make a way to escape, that ye may be able to bear it."

You see, there is a light in the storm. Just look for it.

I have compiled a list of power scriptures to memorize in this book. I want you to learn them and hide them in your heart to grow by. They are also in the front of the book, but I needed to mention them here.

David said in Psalm 119:11, "Thy word have I hid in my heart, that I might not sin against thee."

Romans 4:17 reads, "He calleth those things which be not as thou they were." You need to start calling what you want.

Job 22:28 states, "Thou shall decree a thing, and it shall be established unto thee: and the light shall shine upon thy ways." Decree a thing and speak to it. Say, "It is mine because of the words you spoke."

John 14:14 says, "And if ye shall ask any thing in my name, I will do it." Ask what you will in his name and believe.

Matthew 16:18–19 reads, "And I say unto thee, that thou art Peter, and upon this rock I will build my church; and the gates of hell shall not prevail against it. And I will give unto thee the keys of the kingdom of heaven: and whatsoever thou shall bind on earth shall be bound in heaven: and whatsoever thou shall loose on earth shall be loosed in heaven." To lose or to bind a thing is to take charge over it. It is in your command.

Matthew 18:19 states, "Again I say unto you, that if two of you shall agree on earth as touching anything that they shall ask, it shall be done for them of my father which is in heaven." To have an agreement of the same faith is to become as one in faith. It is faith.

These power scriptures are faith-building scriptures, meant to build up your faith and confidence in the Lord and yourself. In time, it will help you return to what we can have in the Lord.

It is our responsibility to get the word of God in us and us alone. I cannot put it in you; only you can do that. We must learn how to apply these verses to our everyday needs and learn what authority we have been given.

Zechariah 4:6 says, "Not by might, nor by power, but by my spirit saith the Lord of hosts." This is the key to all our success in the Lord. It's not what we are but what we are in him. The Lord has no respecter of person, but he does have a respecter of faith.

Hebrews 11:6 reads, "But without faith it is impossible to please him: for he that cometh to God must believe that is, and that he is a rewarder of them that diligently seek him."

John 4:24 states, "God is a spirit, and they that worship him must worship in spirit and in truth."

The Bible tells us the rise and downfall of man. We can see where the prophets rose and fell. We can also see where we've rose and fallen in the Lord. Many of us live way below our potential as a child of God. Goodness and grace are upon us if we just take it.

I understand some of us have a lot of problems from day to day, but I believe this book, if studied with an open mind and a willingness to overcome problems, will help us grow in faith and power. I know it will not be an easy road, but I believe you will make it if you try. Quitters never win, only those who prevail. So let's prevail in God's riches and grace.

Chapter One

PRAYER OF DESPERATION

Desperation is the loss of our ability to think, wallowing in our own pity and sorrow and the falling in despair of oneself. Desperation is a destroyer of the spirit, a knife that opens the heart to destruction, and a killer of man's will. It is the motion that starts the wheel of depression to set in with no hope in sight. It's the loss of strength and courage. The shame of failure taints love and compassion.

These are the signs of desperation, my brother and sister. This is the silent killer of man's will and soul. So many people in our churches right under our noses are in that kind of shape, and we don't even know it. Maybe it is something brought on by a death, loss of trust in a loved one, or hurt in a church. The list can go on and on.

Desperation, the killer of man, will have no respecter for persons. Take your eyes off the Lord and on your problem and see what happens, my friend. The power of desperation sets in, and I will say the *power* of desperation because it has power. But it only has power if we let it.

Why so many people fall into this situation is much to be discussed. There are three reasons why I believe so many fall into desperation. There are more than three, but I believe these three things are the greatest reasons why we sometimes fall into desperation:

- Not knowing the true word of God
- Not understanding the God-given power within us
- Not knowing how to fight with the word of God or standing firm

List three ways that desperation can come in. List three ways to keep it from coming in again.

The mind is a funny thing. In one moment, it can believe, and then in a second, it can doubt and get really hysterical about a matter. We can rejoice in one breath and be sad in the next.

Not understanding who we are is one of the greatest killers of man I know. You have to know who we are to receive. If you understand your privileges, you must understand the power given to you and how to use it.

Understanding the power within still doesn't make you a fighter in the Lord. You have to see the word and take it for what it is. Know how to apply the word to the situation in need and understand it is truth and no lie. Romans 3:4 says, "God forbid: yea, let God be true, but every man a liar; as it is written."

The only thing that is truth is God's word. But to see it is true is not enough. We have to learn how to see it and apply it to our situation. All three of these go together, and not one is left out. We must first know the word is true and understand what authority we have. We must know the power within or what power we have been given and next know how to apply the word or fight with the word of God. This is the key to the situation, so let's learn how to apply it.

If you understand your privilege, you understand what it is. Explain. List three to see God's word as it is.

The story of our pain and suffering is so different in each one of us that, if we were to tell our story, they could write a novel. But most of us had rather keep our pain and suffering a secret, not wanting anyone to know. But pain is something like a sore that can venture up at any moment without a moment's notice. Not understanding and broken down by the weight of that pain and abuse, we seem to fall backward into a hole of sorrow, wondering, *Why me, old God? Why me?*

I am sure of one thing: There is pain and suffering on every side of us, and none of us is exempt.

Sometimes pain comes from many angles. Not knowing why, but the words are *rejection*, *absurd*, and *unintelligent*. You feel insecure and hopelessly lost, wondering what's wrong with you. You made a bad mistake in your life; people are talking about you. These things and words go to the inner part of the heart to destroy your spirit.

I do not understand why some can get strength over their problems and others can't. I just want to say that God knows why. As people of God, we must fully turn our problems, whether great or small, over to him. I am guilty of such, holding on to incidents that hurt me badly, and still to this day, it almost gets the best of me, making me want to give up. But I know I have tried and fallen many times, but I still maintain.

I want to tell you a story that happened in my life, which I have had many I care not to speak about at this time, but God is true, no matter what.

I got up Sunday morning to go to church and asked my wife, Brenda, if she wanted to go. She said no, so I got ready and left to go somewhere to church, but not knowing where.

As I was driving to Jacksonville, North Carolina, I told the Lord, "This is my last day of serving you. I am going to church and will try to enjoy it, but when I get back home, I will lay down the Bible and never pick it up anymore. But I will still love you, Lord."

All of a sudden, I stopped at a black church. Remember, I was telling the Lord my plans and crying all the way there, not knowing where I was going and what church I would stop at. Then suddenly I stopped at a black church and went in, telling the Lord the whole time what my plans were and how I was going to quit, but how I still loved the Lord.

When I walked in, I planned to sit in the back row. I just wanted to slip in and out. But to my amazement, it was all full. The preacher said, "Brother, there is a seat in the first row."

I walked up and sat down all depressed and sorrowful that this was my last day serving my Lord Jesus Christ. As the preacher preached, he stopped about the middle of his sermon and said, "Brother, stand up and pray for that girl in the back. She has a big tumor in her stomach."

I jumped up and turned toward the back. The lady had stepped out in the center of the aisle. I just said, "Be healed in Jesus's name." And she fell backward. No one caught her. She just lay flat down as if an angel had laid her down, and everyone could see her stomach go down. Everyone was rejoicing, and the Lord said, "What do you think now, son? Are you going to leave me now?"

I said, "No, Lord," and wept all the way home, begging for forgiveness, and from that day to this one, I have never done that again. You see, we all go through things, but he is always there for us to deliver us.

Look at the story of Jehoshaphat when bad news came to him. Jehoshaphat did what we have to do in a moment of desperation, that is, he "called on God." Jehoshaphat said in 2 Chronicles 20:7, "Art thou not our God, who didst drive out the inhabitants of this land before thy people Israel, and gavest it to the seed of Abraham thy friend for ever."

Jehoshaphat had only been king for about two years. During this time, he went through Judah and took away the high place of groves in 2 Chronicles 17:6. He said in 2 Chronicle 17:8–9,

> and with them he sent Levites, even Shem-a-i-ah, and Neth-a-niah, and Zeb-a-di-ah,and Asa-hel,and She-mir-a-moth, and Je-hona-than, and Ad-o-ni-jah, and To-bi-ah,Tob-ad-onijah,Levites: and with them Elish-a-ma and Jehoram priest. And they taught in Judah and had the book of the law with them and went about throughout all the cities of Judah and taught the people.

Jehoshaphat turned the people of Judah back to God by sending men throughout Judah, proclaiming the law of God. The surrounding kingdoms became fearful and made no war with him for two years. 2 Chronicles 17:10 said, "There was piece in the land."

But remember, the devil had not forgotten Jehoshaphat, and neither has the devil forgotten you. The battle will come when. I do not know when, but it will.

When Jehoshaphat got word that a great army had already entered his country to destroy him, it says in 2 Chronicle 20:1, "It came to pass after this also, that the children of Moab, and the children of Ammon, and with them other beside the Ammonites, came against Jehoshaphat to battle." You can see why Jehoshaphat was fearful when the enemy was coming against him. When battles come our way, we get fearful, but the lesson to learn here is what Jehoshaphat did.

Jehoshaphat remembered what God had done in the past for Israel. He reminded God that he was the God and all-powerful and that what he'd done in the past, he would do for him.

You must remember where God has brought you. Lamentations 3:21 says, "This I recall to my mind; therefore, have I hope." Always look back to see where God has brought you, and I believe you may be surprised at yourself when you see where he brought you.

Look at the desperation brought to Jehoshaphat after hearing of the many armies ready to come down and destroy him. 2 Chronicles 20:3 says, "And Jehoshaphat feared, and set himself to seek the Lord, and proclaimed a fast throughout all Judah."

The first thing Jehoshaphat did was call for a fast throughout all of Judah. Why was it so important for him to call a fast upon the people? It was a way of cleansing and a sign of discipline. Fasting is very important to God. Jesus said in Matthew 17:21, "This kind goeth not out but by prayer and fasting."

You will not be delivered from some things until you have prayed and fasted. I know that sounds hard, but it is one of the conditions we must meet to be delivered from some battles we have to face. As you can see, the first thing Jehoshaphat ordered for Judah was a fast.

> And Jehoshaphat stood in the congregation of Judah and Jerusalem, in the house of the Lord, and before the court. And said Lord God of our father, are not thou God in heaven? And rulest not thou over all the kingdom of our heathen? And in thy hand is there not power and might, so that none is able to withstand thee? (2 Chronicles 20:5–6).

Jehoshaphat reminded God, "You are the God of power and might. Are you the one that promises our people through your prophets that, if they would call me, I will hear?" Jehoshaphat knew the promises of God. He stood on what he had been taught, and he stood firm. We need

5

to follow the same lead in times of crisis and trust in God the same way Jehoshaphat did, being confident that he hears us. He did it before; he will do it again.

Now sometimes we find ourselves in the midst of a storm raging out of control. We're trying to overcome! There's no victory in sight! Only more pain and no help can we see. Our mind is in a mess. All the scars we have hidden inside have come back to haunt us. You seem to be quite broken, but help is on the way. Do as Jehoshaphat did, call on the Lord.

List three of the greatest things Jehoshaphat did when in crisis. Can you apply what he did to your situation?

I want to mention different types of problems we sometimes face.

1. Stress (causes) job, sickness, debt, and family.
2. Abuse (causes) hitting, pushing, and being locked outside.
3. Verbal abuse (causes) children, spouses, coworkers, and relatives to belittle you. For example, "You are fat. You're ugly. Can't you drive?"
4. You (cause) feelings of depression, loneliness, being shut out for no cause, or worry, all for no cause.
5. Insecurity (causes) feelings of weakness by peers or abuse. Examples of insecurity are not as pretty, smart, or rich; a bad home life (drunkard home you're ashamed of), and fear (of failure).
6. Mistakes you have made (cause) adultery, lying, stealing, abortion, abandonment, and going to prison.

And the list goes on and on. There can be no end to the list of things affecting your mind, health, and self-esteem. As these words enter your spirit, it is like a cancer that eats away at your desire, hope, and dreams. If not dealt with, it will destroy you over time and cause you to lose out on God.

Words are spirit, and words are life! Words can lift you up to tear you down; words are the entry into your mind and spirit. And words are a way of life. We must watch what we hear. Words are life and will enter into the mind and spirit. Positive thinking is one of the keys to defeating inappropriate words that have no meaning but to tear you down and destroy you.

As Jehoshaphat feared what was upon him, he did not let the words of the great army encamping about him tear him down. He took an approach of "Look at what my God has done in the past and look at who my God is now." Jehoshaphat kept a positive attitude toward the situation about him.

I understand that some people have more problems than others do and others do not know how to get a hold of the truth and victory. But we must learn how to deal with the problem by the word of God.

Now this area of positive thinking and positive speaking is beneficial to us, teaching us how to overcome our problems. The power of positive thinking is not just something we do once in a while; it is a way of life. Keeping a positive attitude toward any situation that comes our way is a great weapon to fight off oppression, postpartum depression, and the battles occurring in the mind.

We need to always stay alert and ready to rebuke any word inappropriate to our hearing. As Jehoshaphat turned to the Lord and asked him for help, so shall we. Look at what Jehoshaphat did when he needed help.

Jehoshaphat turned to the Lord and reminded him, "and in thine hand is there not power and might, so that none is able to withstand thee?" This was the prayer of Jehoshaphat. He wanted to know, "Is not this God that I serve, who has power over all things and who looks after his own?"

Yes, he is the God who is over all things, and he is looking over you now, waiting for you to call upon him in the hour of your distress. He is the God that answers prayer. Matthew 7:7–8 says, "Ask, and it shall be given you; seek, and ye shall find; knock, and it shall be opened unto you: For everyone that asketh receiveth; and he that seeketh findeth; and to him that knocketh it shall be opened."

All you have to do is ask Jesus for it, seek Jesus for it, and knock at Jesus's door, and he will answer.

Is the power of positive thinking and positive speech a way of life? Explain how.

When you recognize you have a problem and you cannot handle it alone, he is telling you to call on him, for he is near. The problem most of us have is that we want to try to fix our problems ourselves, but to no avail.

The problem with that approach is that it might get better for a season, but it will soon rear its ugly head again. As we travel through life, those dark secrets will come back again to haunt us, to try to destroy us again.

The abusive words, the feeling of despair, the pain of insecurity, and the loneliness will just come back and destroy us if we are not careful. God is calling you to deliverance now. So we must learn how to get victory and relief over these pains. We have to go on to victory in the Lord.

Pain is measured in different levels of degrees, and some of the problems we go through are very painful and unbearable to even talk about. And every time it comes back, it gets harder and harder to overcome. We must put up a fight to win, or it will destroy us. I do not understand why we are more vulnerable to the past than at other times, but we are. I do not understand why I can go for months and even years without having any problem over some things and then suddenly there it is again.

All through life, there are conflicts we will have to encounter. Will we hold on to the promises of God so we can overcome them? Matthew 10:29–31 says, "Are not sparrow sold for a farthing? and one of them shall not fall on the ground without your father. But the very hairs of your head are all numbered. Fear ye not therefore, ye are more value than many sparrows."

We are very special to God, and he knows our every need. But even with that said, we still must bear our own burdens from time to time. It is unpleasant, but I firmly believe it is a way of growth. With every trial, there is strength. When we can walk through the fire of the devil and then rejoice, we can say we have grown in the Lord. Psalm 55:22 says, "Cast thy burdens upon the Lord, and he shall sustain thee: he shall never suffer the righteous to be moved." God is going to test us, but you shall not be moved, for he is with you.

Isaiah 5:8 states, "For my thoughts are not your thought, neither are your ways my ways, saith the Lord." Neither is my understanding of why we must go through the same trial so many times, but God knows what he is doing. So let's just let him work in us and go on to victory and live in joy.

Pain comes in many forms and colors. But what do you do with the pain? When in distress, can you apply Psalm 55:22 to you, and can you receive it? Explain.

We have to let the power of positive thinking take over our minds, thoughts, and speech. With the power of positive thinking, we will overcome all our opposition and begin to live a victorious life, but we have to live with that frame of mind every hour.

Positive thinking is a way of talking and thinking, both combined together into one word, happiness. And I know when we walk in a positive attitude, we are happy and smiling, and we are singing songs unto the Lord and our God.

How can you get over this mess and begin to walk in the power of victorious living? Remember what Jehoshaphat did. He did not panic at the news of the great army coming, but he held to what he knew. He was fearful, yes? But he held to the promises of God, and so must you.

I believe he lived an attitude of positive thinking. Jehoshaphat lived with an attitude of "I know my God is with me, I know I shall prosper in my God, I know I shall overcome with my God, and I know I have favor with my God."

What helped Jehoshaphat keep his cool in the midst of this great test? List four ways to overcome and explain why it works.

I just believe he had the right frame of mind, so he did not panic under pressure. Remember 2 Corinthians 1:4, "Who comforteth us in all our tribulation, that we may be able to comfort them which are in any trouble, by the comfort wherewith we ourselves are comforted of God."

Do you see what Paul is telling the Corinthians? We will be in tribulation from time to time, but the same comfort we have received from God, we are to give to others in distress because we have overcome. In other words, the same consolation and help you have received from God and others, we are to give unto others. It is up to you to do unto others as God has done unto you. Matthew 10:8 says, "Heal the sick, cleanse the lepers, raise the dead, cast out devils: freely ye have received freely give."

What if Jehoshaphat had panicked and ran around saying, "What are we going to do? The enemy has come to destroy us." What do you think would have been done to the Israelite people? It would have destroyed them. Yes, it will destroy the next one too.

When going through a trial, you need some reassurance, not panic. What if you were to tell me, my God, "You are in a mess, and I don't know what you are going to do"? I would be astonished! When I was looking for a word of consolation, not a word of despair, God called all of us to depend on him to take the same comfort he has given unto us through our tribulations to comfort others with the words of assurance, not the words of doom.

Tribulation is defined as great distress or suffering by Webster's Dictionary. We all go through different things, some great and others not too great, but no matter what the problem, we, as people of God, have to learn how to apply the word of God to every situation. We are weak at times, but he is strong. The more wood on the fire, the more fire! The more coals you put on the fire, the brighter the light. As you can see, we need one another. No man lives to himself, and no man dies to himself.

Explain tribulation. What do you do in tribulation? Give at least three answers.

In the following chapters, I will explore how to get our minds back in the right direction. I will break down many scriptures that will show you what to think on and how to train our minds to think. We will discuss the power of positive thinking and positive talking as well as believing and the power within you. Jehoshaphat had the power of positive thinking and positive acting. He acted on what he had been taught and what he knew. The power within is a very powerful thing if we learn how to apply it.

Learning how to apply this way of thinking is strange to many, for it is easier to think negatively than to think good things. As a child, we were taught how to walk and ride a bike. Well, we must be taught how to train ourselves to think on good thoughts all the time. It's really not that hard, but you will have to work at it to obtain its goal.

I have to say something, and I hope it does not offend you, but I'm afraid that some of us don't want to get rid of our problems because it is like a crutch we walk with. If we were to get healed, we would not have anything to talk about. I say God is ashamed when we, as children of God, want to wallow in self-pity and our sorrow. God helps us get a grip on ourselves and out of that mess.

I know that some of you are asking if I have ever had any problems. Yes, with a big yes. I have had all kinds of problems in my life, but I'm learning how to deal with them one day at a time. I have not won the battle over all of them yet, but at least I'm working on them. Listen, you are a failure if you don't try. Winners never quit; they only succeed. If you don't succeed the first time, get back up and try again because quitters never win, only those who get back up and try again.

Let's get a hold of the word of God and grow together so we all can be victorious in Christ Jesus. It is up to you and me, and we can win. Life is too short for us not just to play church and not use the potential that God has given us through Jesus's name. In the midst of all our trials and conflicts, we have to hold on to the blessings and promises of God. It's the lifeline of our blessing and strength. With fuel in your car, it cannot run. The same is for us.

Have you ever just sat around and begun to think of all the things the Lord Jesus has done for you with all the miracles he has given you and the protection you receive from him? Most of us never think about that. We want the blessing and protection but never remember it anymore. Jehoshaphat did. He remembered and spoke to the Lord our Father, reminding him of what he had already done. And you will need to if you are to grow in the Lord.

Can you overcome your problem? How?

11

Chapter Two

LISTENING FOR THE VOICE OF THE LORD

In times of desperation, we must listen for the voice of the Lord in every situation we have. The Lord wants us to trust in him and believe his word. Isaiah 55:6 says, "Seek ye the Lord while he may be found, call upon him while he is near." As you call upon him, all heaven rejoices.

Hearing the voice of the Lord is very vital to us. When we are in a state of mind of worry and disbelief, we cannot hear the voice of the Lord. Our ability to think positively has vanished. Then we begin to feel as if we are alone with no one to help. But we are not alone. We are in this thing together, and we are going to win together.

What is the voice of God, and where does it arise from? It is the word of God; it's the still voice you hear inside you. Or maybe he is speaking to you in a vision you've had. You have to learn how he talks to you individually on your own.

I have had many visions that have warned me about some trial or test I would have to encounter. And I have had dreams that would warn me about who I would associate myself with. Every which way God desires to speak to you, no matter which way he chooses, you still have to listen to the voice in a dream or vision or through the word. You have to listen for yourself and see what he will say unto you.

Sometimes God tries to get you to do something for yourself or somebody. The voice of God to some is one way and another way to another. You need to listen to how he speaks to you and watch for it. Look in Habakkuk 2:1, "I will stand upon my watch, and set me upon the tower, and will watch to see what he will say unto me, and I shall answer when I am reproved." Habakkuk is saying, "I am going to sit here really quiet and listen for the voice of the Lord to see what he has to say to me, and when he has spoken, I will answer him."

To hear the voice of the Lord, we sometimes have to get in a really quiet place to ourselves, alone, waiting for his word. But I will say there are times when he will speak when there's a lot of confusion and tumultuous around us. He always sees his children and looks after them.

There have been times in my life when he has spoken to me and would say, "Watch what you say." And sure enough, I would find myself in the midst of some people trying to set me up by dragging me into a discussion about some brother or sister in the Lord.

On one occasion, I was in a revival with some of my friends, and as I started to walk out the door to go home, one of the brothers said, "Brother Jerry, come here a minute."

The Lord said, "Watch what you say."

As I walked over, one of them asked me, "What do you think about the sermon tonight?"

Suddenly the words came out of me, and I spoke. "You know what, brother? There's going to be some in heaven that you would never have thought would have made it, and there's going to be some that don't make it that you thought for sure would make it." Then I said, "Goodnight, brother. See you later." And I left.

What am I trying to say to you? Know the voice of God.

How do we hear the voice of God? Where do we hear it?

I want to give you another example of why it is so important to know the voice of God. My wife and I were having prayer in a church one night. It was on a night set aside just for prayer. On this night, twelve people there were praying.

One of the brothers said, "Let's anoint a cloth on behalf of our good brother and sister in the Lord who are in need."

As the brother got the cloth, we started to anoint it. The Lord spoke to me, "Have each one put their hands, one on top of the other, for a miracle as twelve disciples."

I spoke to the pastor and asked if we could put our hands on top of one another, as the Lord had said. We did so, and the most amazing thing took place that I had ever seen among twelve heads at one time. As we put our hands upon one another with the anointed cloth under the bottom and as each hand was placed upon the other, nothing happened, but when the last hand was placed upon the other, the Holy Ghost came in and spoke through him and went all the way around the circle, speaking through each individual one at a time.

In other words, the Holy Ghost sat upon all twelve, one at a time, to manifest him to us. He spoke in a heavenly language through each one of us, one at a time, each individually. The Holy Ghost spoke four words through each of us, all in a different language. There was complete reverence for the Lord as he moved that night.

But hear the reason I am telling you this. The preacher's wife told me later that night that it had come to her mind to ask us to place our hands one upon another, but she did not ask it. About that time, I spoke up and asked if we would do it. I told her God is an on-time God. He moves, and if we don't move with him, we miss out. That's why we have to listen and obey. I'm glad to say my boy got saved a little later in that same church and is still going on for the Lord.

I hope you can understand why we have to know the voice of God. Remember, if I had not obeyed that night, we would never have seen the great power. In fifty years, they said they had never seen anything like it before. 1 Samuel 15:22 says, "Behold, to obey is better than sacrifice."

List the ways the voice of God comes in.

As you see, we must learn how the Lord speaks to us, whether through his word, with his voice, or in a vision. The voices are the same, no matter which he desires to use. It's still his voice, so listen and learn.

Learn the power scriptures, meditate on them, and pray them, saying, "Now, God, this is your word, and you cannot lie. So bring to pass my blessing in your Son Jesus Christ's holy name." As we practice this, we will begin to see the power of positive speech. Positive thinking takes over our life and restores us to faith again.

Let's not be fooled. It is not easy to live in total faith and dedication all the time, but we must strive for it, no matter what cost we have to bear, whether it be with criticism, mockery, or abuse from others. We have to make it, for the Lord is calling us to such a task. So now let's go forth and be what we are supposed to be in Christ.

Chapter Three

POWER OF POSITIVE THINKING

I want to enter an area that is controversial to some and accepted by others. I firmly believe in it, which is why I speak on it so much. There will be several chapters concerning this subject ahead in this book.

I know that thinking with a positive attitude all the time is hard for some of us. For some of us, we find ourselves struggling to keep us in one frame of mind, especially for a very long time. We are in this frame of thought one minute and in another frame the next. We struggle and struggle to think about good things, and to our amazement, we can only hold that frame of mind for a little while. The next thing we know, we have returned to thinking about all the things bringing us down from the start. But we try so hard to hold on to good thoughts, but to no avail, one minute feeling peace all over you and then feeling despair and hurt next.

I want to tell you we all have a battle with the past and the ghost that is in our life. But the Bible says in Psalm 91:15, "He shall call upon me and I will answer him: I will be with him in trouble; I will deliver him, and honor him." The Lord has said to us,

1. "Call upon him."
2. "I will answer him."
3. "I will be with him in trouble."
4. "I will deliver him and honor him."

Notice the only one in this universe with the right to say "I will," as none other but God can. He has said "I will" three times and mentions the word *him* "four time speaking of you."

This tells me that God is there all the time, waiting for us to call on him, and he said he would answer thee! Note this in your brain. Know that he will do what he said. He will, for he is a God that cannot lie.

As you can see, we have to learn how to control the way we think about ourselves. You must live believing in yourself. If you can't believe in yourself, it's kind of hard to believe in something else. The most successful people in the world will tell you they believe in themselves and what they were doing was the reason for their success.

What are the three (I), and what are the four (Him)?
Name each of them and explain what it is to you.

I will go into the subject of the power of positive thinking later, but I must first build you up to where you understand the prayer of desperation and how Jehoshaphat had the power of positive thinking and power of positive speech. As you can see in the first part of this book about Jehoshaphat, we learned what Jehoshaphat did when confronted with a conflict. He called on God and did not panic at the problem, but kept a level head throughout all of it. Keeping a cool head, even when in fear, kept Jehoshaphat from buckling under the pressure of the conflict. He also knew who he was in the Lord.

When in conflict, we must learn how to keep ourselves and our thought process. When confusion in the mind bogs down the thought process, we are in a vulnerable state of defeat. That's when we, as people of God, find ourselves with no desire to win. Losing is very present in our minds and attitude, all because we do not have control of the thought process in our minds. Remember, the thoughts in our mind are very important to us. It's part of the way we feel, act, respond to one another, and communicate in our daily affairs, and it is very important in the way we appear as Christians to the world.

List and explain five things that can affect your
faith and how you feel about yourself.

We must take hold of this thought process and begin to grow in the Lord. The mind starts the wheel rolling to convince you that you are a failure. But that is a lie! You are going over in Jesus's name now. You may need a little coaching to get you over the hump, but we will help you there.

When we begin to learn that we cannot fight our battle alone, our healing process has begun, and we are on our way to victory. We are not to bottle up our feelings and let them destroy us, but we are to live our life to the fullness, loving our Lord, family, and all those around us. As God asked Cain, "Where thy brother?" we also are to ask where our brother is. We must care for others as we care for ourselves in fellowship with him with a Christ-like spirit. As we begin to learn how to train our mind in positive thinking, we will see ourselves grow in faith and loyalty to one another.

What is the killer of the spirit and mind? List at least five.

Desperation is a terrible thing when it's running wild and out of control. The pain of the past seems to haunt you, and you don't know what you are doing. It is then you have to say, "I need help."

Desperation is good if you go about it the right way. It can put you in a position where you must trust the Lord. So let's do the right thing and call on God to help us and ask a friend to come along as well. Remember the old saying, "Two are better than one." There is a lot of truth to that. And we need to take heed of it.

Is desperation good for you? Explain.

The tension brought on by not being able to handle these problems sometimes can be hard. Sometimes we just need a friend to talk to. Now, that sounds odd, talking to a friend about your problems, but believe me, it works. It's like you are looking for someone to just help with some answers. Or maybe you're looking for someone to agree with you, even though you know the answer will be the same. Clarity is very important to some of us, and it's the fulfillment of an empty spot in our lives. And I know that we did not cause all the problems we face. To some of us, the pain is so draining and unbearable that we have a hard time trying to cope with our problems, much less trying to talk to someone about it. But we need to learn how to open up and let others in. James 5:16 says, "Confess your faults one to another, and pray one for another, that he may be healed."

Sometimes our healing will not come until we have confessed it to a friend and prayed for a friend. Maybe there is something you will have to do first before you are completely set free from that issue. I don't say confess your fault before the church, but examine yourself thoroughly, and you might find an answer. Sometimes forgiving someone who has betrayed you will deliver you from the pain of abuse.

Define clarity in your life. List as many as you want to. Explain what clarity is to them. Explain it.

I understand the positive approach to our problem is the way to go, but some cannot handle it. Either they are weak in their own self-discipline and have nobody to help them, or they are looking for clarity in the situation and want to let it go but just can't. I have been there myself at times and fell back into it again, looking for truth I already knew. But willing to hold on to that problem, I was dragging myself down into that same mess again and again. Not willing to let go, I found myself in all kinds of delusion and frantic state. As I began to pray and ask God, "Why can't I get over these issues I'm having?" he kept saying, "Trust in me and cast all your cares and burdens upon me, for I care for you."

Psalm 55:22 says, "Cast thy burdens upon the Lord, and he shall sustain thee, he shall never suffer the righteous to be move." What a verse that is, to know we will never be moved by anything but our own will to quit.

As you can see, that is easier said than done. So I began to fast and pray and beg God for help over some issue I never wanted to talk about. As I was praying and looking into myself, I discovered some things. And I did not like what I saw. As I pondered over those things, I began to realize I hindered my healing. That is, we need to look at ourselves first before looking at others.

That's not to say that someone else didn't cause your problem because they most likely did. But we have to search ourselves first before looking unto another. As we go through this book, you will get a better understanding of how you can defeat that demon haunting you day and night and start living.

Can you look into the mirror and see where you need to start your healing? Let everyone look and explain what they see.

In this book, I intend to bring all who read and take to heart what they are reading so they will grow in Jesus. All my life, I have seen the devil trampling on children of God. Do not forget that family, friends, coworkers, and, of course, your own self can hurt you as well. It is in every church and home, and every Christian must deal with it in some form or another. But we are children of God, one who cares. We have to get a handle on the situation we sometimes get ourselves in. Sometimes it's our fault, and other times it's someone else's. But regardless, we have to stand on the word of God and overcome the situation, no matter whose fault it was.

Life is too short to live below our means, which is saying it has all been given to us through Jesus. All we could ever want or ask for, just to trust him and live for him with all our heart, is in reach. The next chapter will dive into the comfort of temptation and will cover in-depth what we as Christians can do if we set our minds to it and trust the Lord to carry us through.

Chapter Four

THE COMFORT OF TEMPTATION

God has called every one of us to prayer, fasting, studying, and the right attitude. As Christians, we have many things to face, but in the midst of them, we are to be Christ-like. Trouble and trials come to all, and no one is exempt from it. 1 Corinthians 10:13 says, "There hath no temptation taken you, but such as is common to man: but God is faithful, who will not suffer you to be tempted above that ye are able; but with the temptation also make away to escape, that ye may be able to bear it."

Listen to what he said. Temptations are common unto man, but I do feel like some of the trials we face are deliberate and spiteful. Look at Corinthians 1:4, "Who comforteth us in all our tribulation, that we may be able to comfort them which are in any trouble, by the comfort wherewith we ourselves are comforted of God."

You see, trials and tests are good for you if you let it be. A test is when you are asked to do something you do not want to do; a trial is when you have to endure conflict. Our own ignorance can bring on trials, but so can a test. No matter the test or trial, God's word said he would bring us out. Let's look at this verse and see what it says. Now look here at 1 Corinthians 10:13.

1. No temptation taken you by yourself (2 Corinthians 1:4). He has comforted us in all our tribulation.

21

2. You will not suffer above that ye are able (2 Corinthians 1:6), and whether we be afflicted, it is for your consolation and salvation.
3. There will be an escape route for you (2 Corinthians 1:10) in whom we trust that he will yet deliver us.
4. That ye may bear it (2 Corinthians 1:5), for as the sufferings of Christ abound in us, so our consolation also abounded by Christ. Consolation is the act of consoling, giving relief in affliction. "His presence was a consolation to her."
5. Make a way for your escape (2 Corinthians 4:8–9). We are troubled on every side yet not distressed. We are perplexed but not in despair. We are persecuted but not forsaken. We are cast down but not destroyed. The way of escape is holding on to Jesus.

Can you understand the term "comfort us in all our tribulation"? Who is comforted through your temptation? Explain how they are helped. Is temptation good for you?

He has it all in the palm of his hand. We just have to trust him and live faithfully. All of us are subject to trials of some sort. We just need to know what to do when it comes our way. So many times, people have turned in the wrong direction and almost lost the battle. We had a chance to see what God could do.

Getting the wrong advice is one of the greatest problems we face as Christians. I know some people mean well, but some mean it for your harm. So we need to be sure the information we're receiving is right for the situation we are in. Some of the things we face cannot be answered just by anyone. We have to have the true blessing of our Father's revelation to help us. I want to say that any time you get a revelation from someone who says God told him, I want you to first try the spirit and see if it is of God. How do I try the spirit and see if it is of God? If it does not agree with the word of God, forget it. If it does not bear witness to what you're going through, forget it.

Remember, your dirty laundry was never intended to be put on a clothesline for the world to see. Your dirty laundry was only intended for you, God, and the one giving you the word to know. And listen very carefully: if anyone starts to reveal to you openly something you know is secret right then, tell them to stop and walk away. I don't care if you are in church or not. It is nobody's business. I know that may sound hard, but as I said, your dirty laundry is your own and no one else's.

It is good to have a friend we can confide in, but be wary of who you talk to. God has intended for us to have friends to worship with, pray with, and even talk with, but as I said, your dirty laundry is yours and no one else's.

But I am afraid that some of us talk too much, and others are stubborn with an attitude of "I can fix it my own self." And because of that attitude, it has destroyed many and brought families down to ruins. Look at Proverbs 16:18, "Pride goeth before destruction, and a haughty spirit before a fall." It is a tragedy for us to get in this kind of shape when so much help is around. Romans 14:7 says, "For none of us liveth to himself and no man dieth to himself." Listen, we are the Lord's.

Whose dirty laundry do you have? Explain. Do you have yours or someone else's?

We act as if we have it all under control and do not need anyone. But face it: we all need someone to talk to, someone to be with, and someone to cry on. Trials are in many colors and unpleasant to look at, and they come in many forms, some small and others just unbearable. You see, no one can go through that for you. You must do that yourself, but somebody can go through it with you. We are occasionally faced with the question, "Do I go through this trial alone, or do I call on somebody to help me?"

Only you and no one else can answer that question. This decision is laid upon your shoulder and it alone. When you decide to ask for help, you've just started defeating the battle. You see, we are somebody and in need of somebody. Genesis 4:9 asks, "Am I my brother keeper?" In this passage, the Lord spoke to Cain and said, "Where is Abel thy brother?" Cain lied to God and said, "I know not."

Cain was trying to hide the truth from God. But nothing is hidden. It will come out eventually, whether we like it or not. God knew that Cain had killed Abel, but Cain did not know that God knew. You see, God knows all things.

As you can see, I need you, and you need me. We are a team united, helping one another in every situation that arises among us. God has called us into a great kingdom. Galatians 5:21–22 says, "But the fruit if the spirits is love, joy, peace, longsuffering, gentleness, goodness, faith, meekness, temperance against such there is no law." This is the duty of a Christian to walk in the fruit of the spirit and to help one another.

But it is hard to walk in the spirit when you're in the biggest battle of your life. And you feel like you are all alone without a friend in sight and your peers are abandoning you. And yet you thought you had a friend, and none were to be found. That's when you are at your best. Why? The spirit of truth is in your ear, and now you can hear the voice of God. Friends are great, but we need to hear the voice of God. To hear God's voice is the taking of all truth and strength we need with all the answers, and he is never wrong.

How does this go with the prayer of desperation? What did Jehoshaphat do first in crisis? What did he do second? What did he do third? Now explain what he did and how it applies to you.

Jesus said in John 15:15, "For I call you not servants; for the servant knoweth not what his Lord doeth; but I have called you friends." You see, we are a friend in Jesus.

I understand entering a relationship with another to discuss some of your problems feels very awkward. But to some of us, that's the only way we can overcome, to have someone to keep us from slipping back into that rut again, someone who will say, "Brother or sister, you will be all right because it is working out" or "I'm here with you."

Just a friend to comfort you! Remember, I need someone occasionally to tell me, "Jerry, listen. That's not right. Get a hold of yourself." We have all been there, if we will just admit it, but most try to hide it, not realizing that you're just digging your way into destruction.

We have to fight many battles in this life, but we can overcome them. Now I said previously some are tests and others are trials, but no matter which one, it is something you have to go through. There are weapons against the spirit, and there are weapons of the flesh. These weapons have come to kill the spirit and the body, if possible, to kill the spirit so you will be out of fellowship with God and weapons to kill the body so you will be off the face of the earth. But listen. Matthew 10:28 says, "And fear not them which kill the body, but are not able to kill the soul: but rather fear him which is able to destroy both soul and body in hell)." John 10:10 reads, "The thief cometh not, but for to seal, and to kill, and to destroy."

As you can see from these scriptures, the devil does not like you, and he's out to do one of three things: to steal your joy, to kill your testimony, and to destroy your salvation for good. That's his only goal in life, but we are smarter than he is. So let's look at some tactics the devil uses on us and defeat him at his own game. Remember the title of this book, *Prayer of Desperation*. That's what we are. We are praying daily for the revelation that will give us insight from being entangled in some trap or pitfall of the devil.

List some pitfalls the devil has tried to throw at you.

Now I want to go into the scriptures and show you some of the devices the devil will use against you. Remember what we have discussed about the positive thinking attitude and how important it is. We have to learn this great concept, or we will be struggling from battle to battle. God has given us the provision, and it is up to us to reach out and take it. I want to go into the scripture and discuss some of the things the Bible says can affect the way we think and live.

I am talking about weapons. Weapons against the flesh "can kill the body," for example, swords, guns, bombs, and so forth. Now the weapons against the spirit (Galatians 5:19–21) are first:

- They can destroy your joy, power of God, reputation or testimony, attitude, friendship, and salvation.
- They will bring the utmost Christian to folly in just a moment.
- They will bring depression and shame to those who it will.
- They are weapons of doom against you.

But, remember, if you do enter this area, Jesus is waiting for you to turn back and call upon him again, and he will forgive you and return you back to your rightful place in him.

Explain what the works of the flesh can destroy. List at least six.

Now let's look at some of those weapons against the spirit in Galatians 5:19–21.

SINS OF DESTRUCTION

Adultery	Fornication	Uncleanness
Lasciviousness	Idolatry	Witchcraft
Hatred	Variance	Emulations
Wrath	Strife	Seditions
Heresies	Envying	Murder
	Drunkenness Reveling	

There are seventeen weapons of the flesh sent to destroy the spirit. But God has given us his spirit to fight off this warfare. I want to quickly comment about these seventeen weapons sent to defeat us. James 1:13–14 says, "Let no man say when he is tempted, I am tempted of God: for God cannot be tempted with evil, neither tempted he any man: But every man is tempted when he draw away of his own lust and enticed." James tells us that most of the trials we go through could be because of the full feeling of our own lust fulfillment.

Examine these seventeen deadly sins. Others cause some of these; you cause others. You will have to decide where you fit in that category.

- Adultery: sex outside of marriage
- Fornication: sex between two people not married to each other
- Uncleanness: the act of being unsanitary; lack purity; indecency; unclean
- Lasciviousness: immoral sexual thought or action; lustful
- Idolatry: the worship of images that are not God
- Witchcraft: the art of sorcery; the use of certain kinds of magical power
- Hatred: person who hate; very judgmental; negative; manipulating

26

- Variance: a difference between conflicting facts; "a growing divergence of opinion"
- Emulation: an effort to equal, excel, or surpass another; work through imitation at times
- Wrath: anger; now anger is an emotion, a state of behavioral conduct
- Strife: lack of agreement; bitter conflict; heated, often violent, dissension
- Sedition: disobedience; rebellion; commotion; uprising; mutiny
- Heresies: an introduced change to some system of belief, especially religion
- Envying: feeling of discontent or resentful to someone else; jealousy
- Murder: unlawful premeditated killing of human life
- Drunkenness: overindulge in biblical terms; intoxicated by alcoholic beverages
- Reveling: to take great pleasure in; celebrating

This completes the definitions of all the sins Paul mentions in the book of Galatians. I hope you have read these definitions thoroughly, and please fill free to look up the definitions again for yourself.

I understand you may be wondering why I mention so many different areas in this book when the title is about the prayer of desperation. Look, the prayer of desperation will knock at your doors. Maybe it's not today, but it will come to your door, and when it does, what will you do? Will you panic, run in circles like you've lost your mind, mad, or out of your mind, or will you copy Jehoshaphat? He was fearful, yes, but he did not lose what he believed in, and that was God, his refuge in the storm. Storms will come, and storms will go.

It may be loved ones who betray you or may be hurt as a little kid. Regardless of the problem, it will come upon you somewhere along your life journey. I guarantee it. No one is exempt. We all are tested in some way or another, and there is no escape from it here on this earth.

Will desperation come to you? How? Explain how some desperation has come. Now explain what you did during the point of desperation.

When I started talking about Jehoshaphat and what he did when faced with a crisis, this led us to where we are at the moment. As you see what he did when he called a fast and reminded God, "are not you all power and there is none like unto him," this is the driving force behind this book, that knowing, "that you know" that he is God and there is none other like unto him. Whether the situation is a battle of armed soldiers, a battle raging in the mind, or a driving lust you can't control, it is all the same to the Lord. When in the prayer of desperation, he wants you to do as Jehoshaphat did, "cleanse yourself and call upon him." Jehoshaphat called a fast and then prayed to God. Jehoshaphat did the right thing, so we need to do as he did.

I know we are in a battle for our life, and I know some of us don't understand what to do in a crisis, but the word of God always has the answer for us. Let's look for the answer now.

Do you know that you know?

That is why I wrote this study book so you can understand how simple it is to live a victorious life. We know our mind is a dwelling place for good and bad thoughts, and we have to decide which road we will take. The spirit of this world is talking to us every moment, trying to deceive us in one way or another. And I know that some of us are fighting a battle of our life.

You wonder why you're slipping back and forth from one extreme to another. This upsets you, and you say, "Lord, I don't want to be like this." Yet you slip into another situation crying all the time, saying, "Lord, help me. I am in warfare."

This is a battle we all have to fight, and it's unpleasant. But there comes a time when you have to turn to God and ask, "What must I do?" He will tell you to trust and submit it all to him, and if you do it, he will turn it all around.

Take this word I am about to speak over you and receive it now.

You are about to meet someone; he will encourage you and lift you up as a mentor to counsel and pray with you. Just be willing to accept whosoever it might be, for God is with you. Just watch who you are with, for he may be the mentor you need. Now receive this word and accept.

Can a battle be good for you? Explain.

We are going to always have battles to fight. But in the midst of this battle, you will gain your strength. If you can look into the test you are entering, you will see it is for your good. As the army learns after each victory, so do we get stronger after each win also. Colossians 1:13 reads, "Who hath delivered us out n of the power of darkness, and hath translated us into the kingdom of his dear son: In who, we have redemption thought his blood, even the forgiveness of sins."

We have been delivered out of darkness and put in the glory of God's light, his kingdom. We are his. The battle we are fighting is his battle because we are in his kingdom. The devil wants you to mess up so it will look bad on God and you and laugh at you. But we are overcomers. Even though I fall, he will raise me back up again.

What kingdom is there? List two types. What kingdom are we in? How did we get there?

Two kingdoms rule. One is the kingdom of light; one is the kingdom of the darkness. We have been taken out of the kingdom of darkness and put in the kingdom of light. Now we have access to everything the Lord has for us because we are his. Call on him. Do as he says and see what happens today!

Chapter Five

CRISES IN CONFLICT

We are about to enter a phase of this book that, I believe, will be the greatest learning experience you have ever learned as far as how to face adversity. We can be in church for eternity and still not know how to face adversity and desperation. We all must face it from time to time in our life. But it's the way we handle the situation that counts sometimes. We're in a panic state where we cannot even think for ourselves. Or are we facing the situation with the attitude of knowing that God is with us?

I have been faced with many adversities in my life, and sad to say, I have not dealt with many of them in the right way, and I fail to deal with some of them in the right way. The situation walks all over me, stomping me in the dirt, ready to give up at most any time. Even I have had victory and defeat in my life. When I began to look back at where I had just come from and how I dealt with those situations, it sometimes made me sick to my stomach about how I made a pure mess of some of them.

Life and its troubles are something to be reckoned with, but in the right way. Knowing how to face a situation is half the battle. The other half is believing God will bring you out of it. The other part of the battle is knowing how to approach the problem in the right way.

The title of this chapter is called "Crises in Conflict." Why? As I have already said, many of us go through a lot of things in this life, and you wonder why it always happens to me. Maybe the Lord is trying to build you into a great warrior for him. The greater the battle, the greater the calling, I believe. I have already discussed what Jehoshaphat did in a crisis, how he approached the situation, where he turned to, and what type of prayer he prayed, things that can influence our way of thinking. I've also discussed that we are our brother's keeper.

We have already covered a lot of ground. But we needed to go this way to better understand how some have been there in their situations and overcome life-threatening situations because, to some, it is challenging. They thought they were done in with no way out. We will now go into this chapter looking for growth in our own spiritual walk.

SIX STEPS TO VICTORY

I have spoken to you about many subjects, some I know you do not understand. And some of these are very controversial in their arrangements, speaking of things such as positive thinking, the need for one another, believing is receiving, power of prayer, the strength within us, and the joy of temptations. These are called the six steps to victory. Why? It shows the area we are weakest in. Sometimes we have to be taught how to head off our enemy, such as what to pray for and how as well as what to think on.

POSITIVE THINKING THE POWER WITHIN: POWER OF POSITIVE SPEECH

Now what is the power of positive speech? Positive speech is the attitude of growth that comes from the heart. As we talk, people are reading us like a book, looking inside to discover what we are made of.

Positive speaking and thinking help us to be able to live a life of victory. Positive thinking is not just a duty; it is a way of life. You live it, and then you will speak it. The ways of the Christian are not without adversity, but through the adversity, you will have to speak positive things. But it first must be in you before you can speak it.

Remember, the most powerful thing you can do for yourself is speak positive things to you and about you. The window controls your attitude and personality. The response to those words you speak determines what person you will be. It is not what happens to you, but what happens inside of you that controls the whole attitude of our being.

Are we able to control our feelings, our emotions, or will we come back with a negative word of disbelief? It is natural to feel let down and cast out when things don't go our way, but speaking the right word over a situation is the greatest way to help yourself. The right word will carry you, and wrong words will hurt you. We must always speak the right words. I want to mention some Bible verses that will help you achieve this goal of positive speaking. That's why I mention the power of positive thinking first; what we hear, see, and read govern the word that enter in the heart. Remember Luke 6:45, "for of the abundance of the heart his mouth speaketh."

Does what go in defile the temple? If so, explain.

I want to tell you a story of my wife and me. My wife isn't the most optimistic type of person. It doesn't matter what the situation is; she tends to expect the worst. I want to show you what I did to turn my wife around.

In 2001, I was sitting at the table while my wife was preparing supper. While she was preparing the table, she started talking about how bad things were and how there was no way God would bring us out of this mess we were in. At that time, we were broke, just barely making ends meet. Our heads were just above the water.

As she was speaking, the Lord spoke to me and told me to get up and take her hand. I did not know what he would do, but I got up and said, "Let me see your hands."

She responded, "I don't know what you want, what you are going to do."

I just said, "Let me see your hand." Then it came to me. As she took my hand, I said, "I want you to promise me that for the next ninety days, you will only speak positive things concerning our situation. And if God doesn't turn it around, I will never, ever say another word about you speaking negative again."

She did promise me she would do it. But for about three weeks, I had to say every now and then to her, "Remember what you promised me." She was about to start speaking those negative words again. Then she would remember and start saying positive things. At the end of two whole months, she was only speaking about those things that were positive to our situation.

All she needed was a little boost to get her out of that rut. That is all some of us need, just a little boost from a spouse or friend to get us over the hump we are in. I urge you to find someone you can team up with and go to for some positive talking, and you will be amazed at how much your life will change. But remember, you have to feed the mind with good words, encouraging words, for you to speak good words.

As in the lesson on the prayer of desperation, we must learn what to do in a situation when the forces of evil are coming in on us. As Jehoshaphat called a fast to bring the people back in unity and back to God, he prayed for himself. Then he reminded God he is the supreme being and none like unto him, "in thine hand is there not power and might, so that none is able to withstand thee?" (2 Chronicles 20:6). He was letting God know, "I know in whom I serve."

Read the next paragraph and see if you know in whom you serve.

Did Jehoshaphat know in whom he served? Did he know in whom he trusted? And did he know in whom he committed all to? Can you answer this question today, or do you have to think about it tomorrow? Look, a lot of us say, "I trust," but when it comes down to the test, do you really?

Jehoshaphat did. If I ask you to get in this wheelbarrow and let me push you across the high wire, would you? Now you just said, "I trust," but do you? How many would trust me? Say it was God who asked you. Would you? But if we are to be completely sold out as we say, "I know in whom I serve," we would be able to trust that person in the wheelbarrow, whether it be God or man. And if we "serve him as we have said," we would get in the wheelbarrow and not hesitate.

To be totally committed is to be totally trusting, and to be totally trusting is to be totally serving. Now Moses stepped to the Red Sea first before he stretched forth his hand upon it, and all watched him, and they went across on dry ground. The point I am trying to convey is that

Moses said in Exodus 14:13, "Fear not—stand still and see the salvation of the Lord."

Witnessing the man who asked you to get in the wheelbarrow after you already saw him go across several times should have been enough to build your faith to the point of trusting him. As with Moses, they had seen the Lord work through Moses many times, so they knew God would do something. But listen, to be short in one area is like the rottenness of an apple. Bruise an apple and see what happens. The very spot that was bruised is where the rottenness will start.

So as it is with our Christian walk. If we are weak in one area long enough, it will spoil the rest over a period. The bad spot will spread into the other area of the apple and contaminate the rest. It is amazing how one little thing dwelled on long enough can draw out other bad areas of hurt and pain to the point that you are now with several problems tormenting you at the same time. Why? The scars we have hidden are like an apple getting bruised. It destroys the rest of the apple, if not taken care of.

Now get up and get in the wheelbarrow because we are going over together. I'll push you, so just ride along, enjoying the view of being above the problem and knowing that someone is for you.

Explain some rotten apples you have covered up in your life. But beware of what you uncover.

How can we live a life of positive attitude and live in victory over our conflict? What is this, and how does it work? Will it work in ordinary situations? Will it work all the time? It is a question that everybody asks from time to time. Yes, it will work all the time and every time, but the ball is in our hands. You are the one who must make it work with the help of the Lord. Positive thinking is what it is. It is the right type of thinking.

We are to think about eight things every day and all day. It is to never leave us; it is like a friend that walks with us. He walks beside you from morning to night, from the setting of the sun to the rising of the sun. This friend will never leave you, no matter what. But the only way he can communicate to you is if you will communicate with him. How is that?

Positive thinking comes and goes as you communicate with it. How is this because the friend is in you? The friend we are talking about here is the spirit of God. The word of God is the friend we are talking about. The word of God goes everywhere you go if you have been born again and have studied your Bible. The word of God will constantly talk to you if you will listen. But listen, you have to do your part. Read it, study it, and meditate upon it. Why? Psalm 1:2–3 says, "But his delight is in the law of the Lord, and in his law doeth he meditate day and night. And he shall be like a tree planted by the rivers of water, that bringeth forth his fruit in his season; his leaf also shall not wither, and whatsoever he doeth shall prosper."

What is the psalmist saying? Keep your mind and thoughts upon the Lord, and you shall be blessed in all your deeds: blessed to prosper, blessed to sing a new song, blessed to be planted by the river of water for nourishment. In other words, think on those things that are good and pleasant, and the days will be joyous.

How can this be? Positive words, the power within, is it a fairy tale, or is it truth? A word spoken in its right place is power, no matter the situation. Look at Proverbs 12:25, "Heaviness in the heart of man maketh it stoop: but a good word maketh it glad." What is this saying? Words spoken in doom and gloom are words of destruction, but a word of greatness brings forth peace and calmness to the soul.

Learning how to walk in this type of mindset is no easy task. Learning how to walk with an attitude of praise and worship thinking, good thought, is one of the hardest things I have ever tried to do. Why? We are fighting warfare against the flesh and the spirit. Satan is trying to sift us one at a time as he tested Peter, so will you be tested?

But the question can be asked: how do we defeat these negative thoughts and our discouragement from time to time? In the next chapter, I mention a scripture I break down into many parts for you to understand how to and what to think on. I will not go into it now since you might get confused. In this chapter, we are discussing crises in conflict. It is just trying to help understand what to do when faced with a conflict. Remember Jehoshaphat, when faced with a conflict, what he did. He kept his cool throughout the ordeal and began to set things in motion to do what he had to do. The most important thing we are to do when faced with a conflict of adversity is not panic.

THE NEED FOR ONE ANOTHER: IS IT A GOOD THING?

What is it, or who should we trust in whom we should help? Remember, the clock is always turning, and so are the torture of the past and the present we have had to face. Just knowing what to do when faced with adversity is a very vital and must-do issue. And knowing who your friends are in times of need is a plus. It is one of the hardest things when we try to pick out someone to be a friend. Why? In the midst of a crisis, we don't seem to think well, and sometimes we get an attitude. That is a dangerous thing, to have someone agree with you when the answer they are giving is the wrong answer but the answer you wanted to hear.

What if Jehoshaphat had panic or fear after discovering the armies were encamped around them and said, "I don't know what to do. I guess we will have to run or give up to the Ammon"? Or what if some of the other leaders approached him and said, "Jehosphalt, we can't win. Let's run or give up"?

Jehoshaphat could have said, "Yes, you are right, so let's give up." That would have made him feel more justified to accept defeat since all agreed. Why? He was already contemplating it. He just needed someone to agree with him. Wrong answer, my friend.

Jehoshaphat knew who he was, and he did not need anyone to tell him what to do, but sad to say, some of us need someone to tell us what to do. Wrong, my friend. You need to answer for yourself and stand on God's word. Advice is great, but always be led by the voice of the Lord.

Now, open rebuke is good if done in the right way. Ecclesiastes 7:5 says, "It is better to hear the rebuke of the wise, than for a man to hear the song of fools." That is saying a lot! In other words, he is saying for someone to tell you the truth is a sweet-smelling honeycomb full of honey. Its nourishment of growth is there and being distributed among you by the receiving of the word of truth.

For example, you can be faced with a serious dilemma, and someone is telling you to go another way you feel is wrong, but due to pressure from him and the panic state you are in, you heed to his voice rather than the voice within telling what I am saying or another way. You want to go a certain way, but almost everyone is telling you to go this direction. Well then, an open rebuke is good for the soul if you heed the wise man.

We need to always look for truth in whatever situation we encounter, but let the words always be truth, no matter how bad it would hurt. What if Jehoshaphat had not been stable and one of the captains of his army had come up and said, "Jehoshaphat, we can't win; there's too many of them"?

If Jehoshaphat had not had a stable mind knowing who he served, he would have given in. So many of us have been talked out of our victory just because we took the time to listen to somebody tell us we could not make it, and before we knew it, we had compromised and started to think like them. At that very moment, we said, "Lord, I can't make it," without even giving the Lord a chance to show you can make it.

In other words, you stop the flow of God's promises and blessings by changing what you first wanted to do in the first place. Hold to what you want to do and believe, knowing you might have to go it alone. But remember, God is always with you, no matter what.

Describe an open rebuke. Explain why the need for true friends is so important. Describe how the conflict would have turned out if Jehoshaphat had panicked. Describe God's plan for this conflict for Jehoshaphat.

The need for one another! Yes. Genesis 4:9 says, "And the Lord said unto Cain, where is Able thy brother? And he said I know not: Am I my brother keeper." We are our brother's keeper. Galatians 6:1 reads, "Brethren, if a man be overtaken in a fault, ye which are spiritual, restore such an one in the spirit meekness; considering thyself, lest thou also be tempted." Well, how about that? You are to watch one another's back and be always there for them, always to encourage them.

Who is this friend we need? It is anyone you can trust in and know they will never betray your secrets and the pain you are bearing. For the record here, make sure who you begin to have as a friend is your friend indeed and not a news-tattler. No one lives by himself, and no one died by himself. We are the Lord.

No one has to be in defeat. We just have to learn what will and will not work for us. Listen, the power of positive thinking and the need for one another are the first two steps in our growth to victory. Study them, apply them to your life, and see the change begin.

I created what I called the believer motto, a group of statements I read and quote for my growth. Read them and apply them to you, and see yourself grow in the Lord and above your problem, as I have. We are supposed to be the head and not the tail. In other words, the problem we have is supposed to be under our feet instead of us under its feet. By standing on the word, whether by yourself or with someone, is where the Lord wants you. He smiles every time you put your total trust in him, for he loves us very much, and we are his children.

I had a preacher cut me down and try to mock me by saying, "You think you are something by quoting so many scriptures."

I said, "No, in fact, no, I don't. In fact, the Lord should take a two-by-four board and wear my behind slap out for not knowing more than I do know."

He turned left like a whirlwind had gotten him. He had gotten jealous, and the devil came out of him, but God shut him up. We are to stand for truth. I told the truth. I should know more about the Lord's word than I do, but shame on me, I'm still trying to grow as much as I can among all the battles I have to fight. In other words, we must stand for ourselves, so let's make our own decisions and let the Lord lead us to victory.

Now getting back to the title, "Crises in Conflict" is a great statement, I must say. When we learn to fight our own battle with God's word and his guidance, we have just moved into an area of growth. In fact, that is what this whole book is about, growth in the Lord. It is about growth in our faith, loyalty, and commitment and how we speak, even in our attitude toward bad situations. While learning how to act during a panic or fearful state, we can still get it together and trust our Lord and Savior to bring us through. Remember to study all the power scriptures in front of the book and pray the scripture as well for growth.

Chapter Six

BELIEVER MOTTO (EXCERPT)

Ask yourself this question:

- What is the occasion your words are fitted for?
- What shall you speak for the moment?
- What words are a weapon against the situation?

  - Great health
  - Great success
  - More prosperity
  - Great favor
  - Overflow of blessing

Things I speak on a daily basis:

- I can do all things in Christ Jesus.
- I will accomplish my goals.
- I am the righteousness of God.
- All blessings follow me.
- I have favor of the Lord.
- I have great health.
- Poverty is a thing of the past.

This is what I believe, for every day I speak these in my prayers as well.

I know it is coming to pass. Now, that does not mean you will not have difficulty because you probably will. But it will be easier to overcome your difficulties using this motto if you practice it, "I am all things in Christ Jesus who strengthen me."

I speak these because I believe I have already received them.

- The words that I have spoken are mine.
- I have them by faith because I have spoken it.
- I claim them now because I have received it.

How is this possible?   Yes! Because

- Notice my mind is made up according to his words. I know in what I believe.
- I feed my mind faith scripture so my faith is alive.
- I feed my mind with positive beliefs, so I think positive belief.

Chapter Seven

BELIEVING IS RECEIVING

What is believing, and what is receiving? Good question. Hebrews 11:1 says, "Now faith is the substance of things hope for, the evidence of things not seen." I may ask my friend, "What is faith? Is it light, is it sound, is it darkness, or is it feeling? Can you see it, and can you taste it?"

Well, if not any of these things, then what is it? It is the substance of things hoped for, the evidence of things not seen. Can you see God? What did God tell Moses when he wanted to see God's glory in Exodus 33:20, "And he said, thou canst not see my face: for there shall no man see me, and live." He also said in the nineteen verses, "And he said, I will make all my goodness pass before thee." In other words, "Moses, you will see my goodness, but not my face."

We see the goodness of God every day but don't see God. Because we trust by faith, I don't see it, but I believe it. The word said it, and I believe it. But does that give you faith? That is good. Romans 10:17 says, "So then faith cometh by hearing, and hearing by the word of the Lord."

Then faith is built day by day by the word of God, and that is faith. You hear it, and you believe it with no hesitation. It was from the beginning and will remain until the end.

Remember, faith comes through the word of God and only through the word. Now there are times when you will see and hear of a miracle that will enhance your faith, but it will not sustain you until you have applied the word of God to you. Reading and listening to the word of God is the only way to receive sustainable faith. You were given a measure of faith from the beginning, but it is not enough to sustain you for the long haul. You must study the word of God daily and apply it to every situation to have great faith. Remember James 1:22, "But be ye doers of the word, and not hearers only, deceiving your own selves." James is saying, "Hear the word, but also do the word, no matter what it tells you to do." Do it, and your faith will grow. If your faith is a little weak, do as the disciples did, ask the Lord for more faith. Luke 17:5 says, "And the Apostles said unto the Lord, increase our faith."

So even the disciples said, "Lord, increase our faith." So if they ask the Lord, can we also? So now ask the Lord to increase your faith and start receiving.

Is faith measured? I was sitting in my rocking chair meditating upon the Lord when I asked the Lord to show me what faith is. As I was sitting there, I looked at my refrigerator door and saw the number from the bottom to the top of the door. The number started with zero as a measure of faith. Then it went up the door from number one to number ten, the largest.

He told me zero is the measure of faith everyone gets from him for accepting the Lord Jesus Christ as his Savior. All the rest are given to you as you increase in faith through reading the word, overcoming trials, trusting God with your issues, living a prayer life, fasting, and dedicating. Then your faith is being increased day by day. Now is fair to all. You may say, "Oh, he has great faith." Yes, he does, but he paid the cost to receive great faith, and so will you.

Faith is nothing to play around with. Why? You can lose it a lot quicker than you receive it. How can that be? By not taking care of it through reading the word and exercising your faith.

As you will see, you will see why faith is so important to God and us. Did Jehoshaphat have great faith, or did he just know in whom he served? He had all of the above. How do I know? If he had not had faith to believe, he could not have prayed such a prayer as he did.

> And Jehoshaphat stood in the congregation of Judah and Jerusalem, in the house of the Lord, and before the court. And said Lord God of our father, are not thou God

in heaven? And rulest not thou over all the kingdom of our heathen? And in thy hand is there not power and might, so that none is able to withstand thee? Art thou not our God, who didst drive out the inhabitants of this land before thy people Israel, and gavest it to the seed of Abraham thy friend for ever. (2 Chronicles 20:5–7)

What a powerful prayer he prayed. Reminding God of what he has promised is stepping into the throne room of God and saying, "God, here's your word. It can't not lie. Now, Lord, honor your word with a miracle." We must maintain a hold on our faith with all our strength and might. If not, we will come up short when we need it.

How big is a mustard seed, my friend? It is so little that it is hard for me to see. But with faith as little as a mustard seed, I can move mountains and cause valleys to be filled and rivers to stop so I can walk across on dry ground. This is the faith that is no larger than a mustard seed. Well, let's jump on board and receive the faith to move mountains. Let's let the world see the glory of our God through us and praise his name.

Have you ever seen a miracle? Well, you are looking at one when you read this book. Why? I was lost and did not care about the Lord in any way, shape, or form. I just did not care one way or another. My wife went to church, and that was all right, but I would not go. One day sitting in my house all alone, looking at the four walls, I picked up a big Bible my wife's mother had given us. I opened it up, and it opened to red writing.

I laid the Bible across my chest and said, "Lord, I always heard the red writing is you talking. Well, I am talking to you now. Lord, forgive me and help me."

And right then I was saved, and I started crying. I did not understand, and all of a sudden, my children came in, and I jumped up, wiped my eyes, and went outside, but I went to my wife's church that following Thursday night and made it known to the church that I was saved at home. I didn't understand why I just did it all of a sudden, and I am so glad.

It's been over forty-four years now, and the Lord called me as he did, and the little seed of faith like the mustard seed we all have opened the door to believe in him with all my heart.

Chapter Eight

THE STRENGTH WITHIN US

James 1:2 says, "Brethren count it all joy when ye fall into divers' temptation." What is this diver's temptation we are to rejoice in? What is this joy of temptation? Joy is the emotion of oneself through one's pleasure. It is also a state of mind or feeling characterized by contentment, love, satisfaction, and pleasure. It's the man standing alone in the middle of adversity and saying, "All right, boys, it will be okay. The Lord will take care of it." He's the one in control of his own life, able to make decisions in the worst of times, for he knows the God he serves has protected him. And because of that, he is joyful. His walk is anchored, and the cross of Calvary is always near to his heart.

Jesus said in John 15:11, "These things have I spoke unto you, that my joy may be in you, and that your joy may be made full." Jesus is saying the same joy he had when he endured the cross for us is the same joy he has given unto us.

With this joy, we are to take rejection and be despised, being put down having all and yet having nothing of this world. Nehemiah 10:8 says, "the joy of the Lord, in your strength."

How can I count it all joy when I am in the worst trial of my life?

Listen to life-changing hands! Before we answer the question, next!

Life is full of bumps. But the way you approach the bump is what counts. If you go over too fast, you might get thrown out of the car. If you are too slow, you might get hung up on the bump, or you might not need to go over the bump at all. Do you understand what I am talking about here? You must go over those bumps just right or bypass them.

Now how is the right way, you may ask? The right way is to first look at the bump and examine it. See if it has any pitfalls or hidden surprises going over it. Well, now you may wonder what a pitfall is. It is a hidden surprise. It can be most anything, like things in the past that do not bother you now but can be triggered by the explosion of another problem you have had. And because of the severity of the problem, the small problem you thought you had conquered now has been resurrected by another issue, and you now have double trouble, all because you went over the bump too fast or too slow when you were to bypass the bump.

Your joy can be snapped away in just a few moments, and you're right back at the bottom again, looking up at the situation instead of down upon it. Bumps of life sometimes are sent to strengthen you, and Satan sends some bumps to throw you. You have to know which one is good for you and which one is bad for you. This is a hard decision for you or anyone to make because there are many avenues to go down. Only you can make that choice, so pray and ask God to lead you on the right path.

Explain some of the pitfalls we can fall in if we are not on guard at all times. Look at what could have been Jehoshaphat's pitfall also.

How in the world can you keep your joy in the midst of this dilemma? The answer is simple! I want to give you three answers to this question.

1. How much do you love the Lord?
2. How much do you love your calling?
3. How much do you love people?

If all of those answers are "a lot," your joy will remain. You may not be able to shout, not even be able to really sing a song, but you will still have joy because joy is in the heart, not in the shout or the

45

song. Don't let that throw you now. Too many of us have jumped and rejoiced in emotion rather than fact, knowing he took you when no one else would have you. The greatest joy of living is to know that your name is written in the Lamb's Book of Life and that no one can take it out. No matter what you have been through, that joy will always remain with you.

If you have said yes to all of the questions mentioned previously, that is your joy, my friend. Yes, rejoicing, shouting, and singing are great, and I love them very much. So keep on rejoicing, shouting, and singing, and be proud to be child of God, but rejoice greater than that. Your name is written in the Lamb's Book of Life.

Do you think that Jehoshaphat lost his joy when the children of Ammon came in around him to destroy them? I think the joy in him was so great that even the fear he had over the word of the Amorites could not stop the joy he had of the Lord. Why do I think Jehoshaphat had joy?

1. Look at the way he confronted God through his prayer.
2. Look at the way he led the children of Israel to prayer and fasting.
3. Look at the way he took control of the situation. He took control.

These three factors and these three factors alone kept Jehoshaphat. Because of these factors, he was able to stand up and proclaim, thus said the Lord in his prayer.

1. He confronted the Lord because he knew what the Lord had done in the past and would do for him in the future, for he knew God was not a respecter of person and this was his joy of knowing he would do it for him also.
2. He confronted the situation by leading the children into prayer and fasting. This also was a way of returning them to unity and peace and turning them away from the conflict beginning to come upon them so their minds would not stray from God's promises. You have to hold on to the promises of God, even through the toughest of times. He also uses prayer and fasting to show God you are ours, Lord. Not only did he lead them to

prayer and fasting, but through it, he brought strength and willingness to stand up for what was right. Look, someone has to stand up, but will joy cause you to stand up in a time of conflict. Why? The joy of the Lord is your strength (Nehemiah 8:10). This is the overcoming factor throughout all of life's difficulties, your joy. You cannot buy it, lease it, borrow it, or even claim it because the Father gives it to you. You had no joy lost then. He came and saved you and gave you joy of peace through him. Now, that is what Jehoshaphat had. He had the joy of knowing that his God, in whom his forefather had served before him, took care of his people and that he would take care of him now, and that, my friend, is joy, the knowing he is with you always.

3. Jehoshaphat came in as a man of valor, stood in the midst of the congregation, and said, "Here's what we are going to do. We are going to fast, pray, and stand together in unity and wait for an answer from the Lord on what direction we are to fight this enemy." Look at 2 Chronicles 20:12–13, "O our God, wilt thou not judge them? For we have no might against this great company that cometh against us; neither know we what to do: but our eyes are upon thee. And all Judah stood before the Lord, with their little ones, their wives, and their children." Look at what happens when they are together in unity and faith. 2 Chronicles 20:14–15 says, "Then upon Jahaziel the son of Zechariah, the son of Benaiah, the son of Jeiel, the son of Mattaniah, a Levite of the son of Asaph, came the spirit if the Lord un the mist of the congregation; And ye said, Hearken ye, all Judah, and the inhabitants of Jerusalem, and thou King Jehoshaphat, Thus said the Lord unto you, Be not afraid nor dismayed by reason of this great multitude, for the battle is not yours, but God's." This is a perfect example of a man who knew where he was always. Yes, fear did come upon him, but it did not overtake him. Why? The joy of knowing the Lord was on his side was his strength, and that's what real joy is, my friend. It is that joy way down in the heart of man.

**Explain the three factors that Jehoshaphat did.
List each one and how you understand it. List what
happened when Jehoshaphat called them together. Did
Jehoshaphat have joy, and how do you know?**

Look at what Peter said in 1 Peter 1:8, "Whom having not seen, ye love, in whom, through now ye see him not, yet believing, ye rejoice with joy unspeakable and full of glory." Peter is saying, "You don't see him, but you love. And yet believing, you rejoice in him, and because of this, you have joy unspeakable and full of glory."

When Peter and John were beat because they preached the word of Jesus in Acts, they counted themselves worthy and rejoiced because they were beaten for the Lord. What kind of joy is this, friend? It is love, yes?

Look at what Paul had to say in 2 Corinthians 7:4, "Great is my boldness of speech toward you, great is my glorying of you: I am filled with comfort, I am exceeding joyful in all our tribulation." Here, Paul is saying, "I am exceedingly glad in your tribulation."

What? How can that be? To suffer for Christ is to gain. But what type of suffering are we talking about here? We will mention two types of suffering, but let's see what tribulation is. Tribulation is defined as "any adversity, a trying time or event." In other words, it is anything we have no control over. If someone were to walk over to you and insult, offend, or scream at you just for doing so and you had not provoked them, that, my friend, is adversity. Two types of suffering I want to mention are suffering of the past (things you have not done or abuse you have lived in) and suffering of your own fault (things you have done you are guilty of).

Note: none of these are tribulations! Tribulation is what I have defined previously. I will say there are some of us that God has chosen to be tested by the devil, as Job was. God allowed Job to be tested by the devil to prove to Satan he would not deny the Lord or cuss him, as the devil said. I know that God has chosen some to go through similar things to prove to the devil that he is God's child and will never turn back. This, my friend, is called tribulation.

Matthew 24 talks about tribulations we all will go through, for example, wars and famine. These also are tribulations. What was Paul speaking about? "I am exceeding joyful in all our tribulation," he is speaking of! To suffer for Christ is what Matthew 5:44 say, "But I say unto you, love your enemies, bless them that curse you, do good to them that hate you, and pray for them which despitefully use you, and persecute you."

Also in John 15:20, it reads, "Remember the words that I said unto you, the servant is not greater than his Lord. If they will persecute me they will also persecute you; if they have kept my saying, they will keep your also."

Do you get the picture now? Paul was saying it is great joy and consolation to know that his brother and sister in the Lord have endured tribulation or trial and still stood for God and our Lord Jesus Christ. Is it a great honor to stand with someone who has stood for truth, no matter the consequences? Paul is saying this brings him great comfort and joy.

What about Jehoshaphat? Did he come through the trial of tribulation in a way that, if Paul had been there to see the situation, he would have had joy and comfort in how Jehoshaphat dealt with it? I believe he would have been happy with how he went about it in every area. Yes, Jehoshaphat was fearful, but that did not cause him to lose sight of the strength of his joy. His joy was knowing that God would never forsake them, and neither will ye forsake you. But now, look at your situation and ask yourself the question. Could Paul say, "I am well pleased with how Jerry Quinn has dealt with some of the trials and tests he has been through"? So the question can be asked, "What do you think about this question, and will you answer it for yourself?" If so, what is your verdict?

What is your verdict on whether Paul could find joy in your tribulation or not, or could anyone?

Notice we are still on the subject, prayer of desperation. Desperation is the loss of our ability to think, wallowing in our own pity and sorrow and falling in despair of oneself. Desperation is a destroyer to the spirit, a knife that opens the heart to destruction, and a killer of man's will. It is the motion that starts the wheel of depression to set in with no hope in sight.

What is desperation to you?

In other words, all through life, there are tests and trials to encounter, but how we deal with those encounters is the key to our success, whether trials of past you are having a hard time with or just abuse from a loved one. The outcome is still the same. All we go through is for the glory of God and for you to gain strength. It is your light shining for the world to see. It is the light of Jesus that is in us that people see and draw them to the light and not darkness.

So the way we are perceived daily is what people see. Is this what we call glorying in ourselves when we are being tested and the world is looking on? Or should we say we will glory in our joy and tribulation and this is our great comfort? Rejoice, my brother.

Romans 5:1–4 says,

> Therefore being justified by faith, we have peace with God through our Lord Jesus Christ: By whom also we have access by faith into this grace wherein we stand and rejoice in hope of the glory of God. And not only so, but we glory in tribulation also: knowing that tribulation worketh patience; and patience, experience, and experience hope: And hope maketh not ashamed; because the love of God is shed abroad in our hearts by the Holy Ghost which is given unto us.

Now, my brother, that is saying a lot! Look, tribulation worketh patience, patience worketh experience, and experience worketh hope, and this hope maketh us not ashamed to go through a trial or to be talked about and cast down because you know he withstood it and so can you. And because of this mindset, we count it joy to have endured such afflictions.

Why is patience after tribulation? Why is experience after patience? Why is hope after patience?

Look at this thought for a moment: To endure adversity is like saying, "The teacher has come." Well, that is deep and probably over your head if you don't think out of the box. To think out of the box is like saying, "I am open to more learning." If you are open to more learning in the word and ready to be taught, then tribulation is about to come. Why? Tribulation worketh experience. Listen, the greatest preacher, greatest teacher, and greatest prophets have endured the greatest affliction. How can this be? Are you stronger and wiser than when you first started serving the Lord? If the answer is no, there's a great problem here.

How do you think Jehoshaphat would have answered the question? Jehoshaphat, are you stronger and wiser than when you first started serving the Lord? I believe he was wiser. He no doubt had seen Judah fight the Amorites and the surrounding armies throughout the country as a little boy and seen the adversity and anguish from the tribulation of war, famine, and sickness. This is tribulation that worketh experience, and experience worketh patience. Look at what Jehoshaphat did. He prayed, called a fast, and waited for an answer from God. No matter what you are going through, you have to pray, fast, and wait for the answer.

When we move without the direction of the Lord, we get in trouble, learning "to let patience have her perfect work, that ye may be perfect and entire, wanting nothing" (James 1:4). The pain and tribulation are for your own good when you can look at it with the right viewpoint. It's not easy to accept everything we have to go through in life as a training, but if we will let the Lord help us, we will be able to grow by our afflictions.

To have patience is to control one's action.

Here is a story of something that happened on a job I work on. Two heads were going behind my back, trying to get me laid off since someone had to be laid off then. They did everything they could to do just that, but I just kept going. On December 10, I was told I was getting laid off on January 20.

I said, "OK, Lord, find me somewhere to go."

In the meantime, the company had a Christmas party. My wife and I went that night, and several said they were sorry they had nowhere for me to go. So we accepted it, but my boss, whom I worked on project with, said, "You are not going anywhere."

I said, "Well, it's already been set."

He said, "No, not going to happen now."

What is happening here is that God will put people in your path just to look after you when you cannot help yourself. My wife and I left that night to drive back, and the next morning, I got a phone call from my boss man.

He said, "Hey, man, start studying for the asphalt and concrete test because you are not going anywhere. The two who tried to get you off the job are leaving."

I asked, "But how?"

He said, "God worked it out for you."

You see, the Lord will use whom he will at any time to bless his people, and I have been doing this kind of work for eighteen years, thank God, because the Lord gave me favor with a man who stood up for me and he will do the same for you. Now let's live for the Lord and take him at his word.

Chapter Nine

POWER OF THE MIND

How in the world does a title like "Power of the Mind" apply to this book title, *Prayer of Desperation*? I hope to show you that we can learn a lot in the study of Jehoshaphat. There are many avenues of man's faithfulness, his dedication to God and his people. Through all of it, we can see different avenues of stewardship we can copy if we try. To grow in the Lord is to grow in grace. To grow in faith is to grow in power. And to grow in desire is to fulfill his will. He desires that you desire him more than anything on this earth. Matthew 6:33 says, "But seek ye first the kingdom of God, and his righteousness; and all these things shall be added unto you." He desires us, but he wants us to desire him.

What is important about controlling the mind?

What was it that Jehoshaphat had above all the other wonderful traits? Was it the powerful prayer he prayed? Was it the way he stood up in the midst of the congregation and brought great unity to the people? Was it the way he asked the people to come together and fast? Or was it when he asked the people to wait and see what the Lord would say unto them? I believe the greatest thing relevant to Jehoshaphat's victory during this terrible ordeal was the power of the mind, knowing God was with him. Why do I think so?

It will be hard for you to fully understand at this time due to this new way of thinking you are about to enter. It may sound like it is new, but it is old. It's been around for ages, since the beginning of time. Positive thinking and positive speech are the same as standing on what you believe or saying what you believe and not wavering from your decision, no matter what. We discuss some of this in chapter three, but here we will dive a little deeper into the power of mindset.

But to walk with this mindset is up to you. Jehoshaphat did. He knew in whom he served and in whom he trusted. But how hard is it to walk with the mind of Jehoshaphat? Not hard, if you are willing to give it all and stand on God's word and just believe what he says. If you can't believe, it will not work that one thing for sure.

What do you see makes you feel Jehoshaphat had the power of positive thinking and power of positive speech? Explain.

There should be at least four answers. Look at the example I gave a class I was teaching some years ago. Write the word *knowing* on both corners of a sheet of paper. Both words were spelled identically, alike. What would this be telling you? This is a good question. What does it mean? Well, this will be a little deep for you if you're not careful, but you can grasp it if you have open ears to receive.

Here, we go with the lesson of the writing on the paper. You have written the word *knowing* on both corners of the paper. Each word looks and is spelled alike, but to two different people, they are different. Now how about that? Spelled alike and look alike but mean two different things. How can that be? The two people who look at it have two different types of faith. One knows God will do it without wavering. The other looks at it and says he knows, but in the back of his mind, he is hearing thoughts like, *Well, I think he's going to do it, if he wants to.* Do you see what I am trying to say? You have to know he is going to do, without any doubt. This he knows without wavering.

In other words, you have to want to always walk with a positive attitude, not being in an up or down mode, as so many Christians. You must enter an area in faith you know he will do it. No one else has to tell you, but you know. You're looking at the paper and reading the word, knowing that God will do it without wavering, no matter what doubt is around you.

Take a piece of paper and write the word *knowing* on each corner on the same side so you can see both words at the same time. Ask each person to look at it and answer it for themselves.

How in the world does the power of positive thinking and the power of positive speech go along with the example I give you about knowing? Think about it. If your mind is not in the right mindset, do you think you will receive anything? No, I can answer that! James 1:8 says, "A double minded man is unstable in all his ways."

You cannot say "I believe" one day and the next day wonder if it will happen. You have to walk it, talk it, live it, and breathe it every day, all day. And this becomes what is known as the power of positive thinking.

Are you unstable or stable? Ask it for yourself. Do you think Jehoshaphat was stable, and would you have done what he did?

Are we going to investigate the power of positive speech and the power of positive thinking as a way of life, or are we going to pass it off as something that is meaningless? To one, it's a way of life; to another, it's just something he's heard about but never tried.

The areas I want to enter currently are the nine steps of victory. Up to this moment, we have covered a lot of ground concerning the prayer of desperation and what it means to us and how we sometimes let situations get us down and out.

The main theme of the nine steps of victory is based on one verse taken out of Philippians 4:8. So I encourage you to read it carefully and apply what you have already studied to this point and add that to it. You cannot understand this subject area unless you can apply what you have been taught up to this moment. To train yourself to think and speak in a positive way has to be a way of life and willingness on your part.

Our life is surrounded by opposition from every side with no mercy to us, as you have seen in the second chapter, "The Sins of Destruction." And in the midst of all, we can find ourselves very vulnerable to those tactics and on the verge of falling backward if not careful. Knowing this, we need to learn what to do when the storm hits us. The key to any of our victories is knowing what to do in times of adversity. Jehoshaphat knew what to do in the situation he was in. Look at what Jehoshaphat did. He called on God, he called a fast, and he called for the assembling of God's people. He called on all to wait on an answer from the Lord.

List the four things Jehoshaphat did. List four things you would have done in the same circumstance. In times of trouble, can you stand? In times of loneliness, can you stand? Will you stand all by yourself, no matter what?

Now as you look at what Jehoshaphat did in times of crisis, you can see it could have only been brought about by the help of God and the power of positive thinking. The power of positive thinking and speaking, I believe, helped Jehoshaphat do the right thing while he was in a time of desperation and fear. His mind was in the right place, the power of the mind.

Philippians 4:8 says, "Finally, brethren, whatsoever things are true, whatsoever things are honest, whatsoever things are just, whatsoever things are pure, whatsoever things are lovely, whatsoever things are of good report; if there be any virtue, and there be any praise, think on these things."

Paul is writing to the Philippians to help them understand that God has a plan for them to live by and to understand that certain laws govern our minds. He wanted them to understand that they were to follow the teachings of Christ and do his will.

He was saying that our minds are to be a place where God can speak and guide us into deeper depths of his word. But I'm afraid most of us are not living that kind of life yet. Because of this, we are tossed to and fro by the sounds of words, and our minds are running rampant all over us.

But, to my confession, I have been there. Many times, I have been where I did not know where I was. The things that were around me and things of the past seem to have infested my head and just filled it with junk to the point I could not carry on. I was mean to family and friends.

2 Corinthians 1:4 says, "Who comforteth us in all our tribulation, that we may be able to comfort them which are in any trouble, by the comfort wherewith we ourselves are comforted of God." As I began to read this scripture, I asked, "How I can comfort others if I am in the midst of my trials?" That's when I realized I had to turn it all over to the Lord, and doing so, he would comfort me in my tribulation. It was trust I had to start doing! By doing that, I would find myself in a position of God helping me through my difficulties. I would have the strength and wisdom to help others and comfort them because I had already been through some similar situations.

Some of us think we can handle all our problems, but sadly we can't. What good would God be if you handled your problems and never asked him for help? If you're on account, you only need God when you can't help yourself. What is that to God? He wants you to trust him with everything, big and small. Song of Solomon 2:15 says, "Take us the foxes, the little foxes that spoil the vines: for our vines have tender grapes."

Notice, little foxes or little things we take for granted might have a great impact on our blessing from the Lord. It might be possible, if you do not trust God in the small things, he may not help you in the big things. Remember, we are as little grapes on a vine, ready for growth. But what happens to a grape that does not get enough nourishment? It dies. When you do not trust God for all your needs, whether great or small, you're not getting nourishment for some critical area of your life.

A great example of that is what we buy. Do we consult with our heavenly Father, or do we go about ourselves as if we are our own boss and don't need his input? I want you to think about that. Is he your God all the time, or is he your God when you don't have anywhere else to go? You decide for yourself and see what your answer might be.

Luke 6:45 says, "A good man out of the good treasure of his heart bringeth forth that which is good; and an evil man out of the evil treasure of his heart bringeth forth that which in evil: for of the abundance of the heart his mouth speaketh." As you see, from the heart our mouth speaks some to good words and others to evil. Feed your heart with good things, and you will speak good things.

There is a word you seldom hear in our churches nowadays, *sanctification*. What is sanctification? Sanctification is the state of growing in divine grace because of Christian commitment. John 17:17 says, "Sanctify them through thy truth; thy word is truth." You may ask how we are sanctified. By the word! In other words, what the word says you trust and what the word says you do. Then you are growing in sanctification. Remember, you will never be totally sanctified holy because it is a daily process we live. It is a total commitment.

God can only impart himself to the receiver if you are a willing participant. The participant is only sanctified by faith when they are obedient to the word of God. To live a sanctified life in the Lord is total dedication to him every day.

I wrote at least three things that had to be done to start the process of being sanctified. There are a lot more than that, but the Lord will show you as you grow in grace, for example:

- What type of friends should I hang around with?
- What places should I hang out at?
- What type of music should I be listening to?

Examples include underground heavy metal and racially-motivated rap music, which I think has lowered our kids and grown-ups down to a level to where they are not producing their level of potential. We need to take charge over the type of music our children listen to. This is my comment and only my comment. I love rock music and play old-time rock music from time to time. That does not make you a sinner for listening to it, but I believe that some of today's music is right from the devil/Satan and has a great influence on our youth. But the question that was asked is that some things you will have to decide on. Is it right or wrong for me? Your conviction will have to play that role.

Let's get back to the study of sanctification and see if we understand what our duties are. Everyone must carry himself, and we must "work out our own salvation with fear and trembling" (Philippians 1:12). This is your calling and yours alone. I have my salvation, and you have yours! You will have to want that kind of life, and if you do, the Lord will meet you there. Remember, he will impart all his blessings, even daily sanctification, to you, but you have to want it.

Isaiah 35:8 says, "And an highway shall be there, and a way, and it shall be called 'The way of holiness;' the unclean shall not pass over it; but it shall be for those; the wayfaring men, through fools, shall not "err" therein."

Look, only you can walk that highway for yourself and no one else. Who are the wayfaring men? They are fools for Christ. Luke 9:23 says, "if any man will come after me, let him deny himself, and take up his cross daily, and follow me." You and only you can carry your cross daily through every event that comes your way, but carry it in the life of sanctification.

What does sanctification have to do with Philippians 4:8 and the prayer of desperation? Look, when you desire to walk in Philippians 4:8, then and only then can you understand the power of sanctification and the power of prayer. Philippians 4:8 will bring you into an area of your Christian walk that causes you to live a sanctified life daily and will build you up in the most holy faith. There is power in that scripture if you let it be, but you have to want it. "Power to overcome those demons some of us are fighting in our minds." It is the word we have to dwell on to overcome. Some of us have battled the past hurt and pain for some time now. We need to get strength over them all, and learning what to think on is very vital to overcoming our problems. I mention thinking positively! Yes, I did because, if we are going to overcome, we have to learn to think positively and practice it daily.

I'm afraid we're living far from our privileges of Christ, and some don't even know it. I say, "Shame on us!" We have to turn back to the old landmark our old forefather has set. Proverbs 22:28 says, "Remove not the ancient landmark, which thy fathers have set." In other words, if sanctification were good back then, it should be good today. But I'm afraid it's a dirty word for some churches of this day.

In the title of this book, *Prayer of Desperation*, why was Jehoshaphat's prayer so important? What did he have that we may not have? What do we need to do to have more faith? It's summed up in two words, *stand* and *believe*.

The power of overcoming victory sums up into sanctification and dedication. Now let's answer the question I asked you to answer. Why was Jehoshaphat's prayer so important? Because of how he approached God, he went straight to the point. What did Jehoshaphat have we might not have? He had a faith approach. Hebrews 4:16 says, "Lets us therefore come boldly unto the throne of grace, that we may obtain mercy, and find help in the time of need." No matter the problem, go to the throne of grace before God and your Lord Savior Jesus Christ to get help.

We find ourselves sometimes bogged down by certain opposition, and we try to get out, but we just don't know how. It is God's great pleasure to help us in any circumstance we may have, but it is our duty to live a life where his blessings will flow, to want the fruits of the spirit to rule in us so strongly that, if someone were to swear at you or lie on you, our response would be, "Lord, forgive them, for they know not what they do, for they are still in darkness." Notice carefully! Without the right frame of mind, the outcome might be different when being lied on or sworn at.

This mindset enables us to say, "Lord, forgive them, for they know not what they do." I'm not going to say you never want to get mad and say things you should not say or even get a little ill with a person, but I guarantee you, if you're walking where you're supposed to, you will not fall as fast. Even I have come short a few times to my shame. But God has helped me overcome each time. We are supposed to be able to maintain ourselves, but sometimes we do come up short, if we will be honest. Jesus is the only perfect one, but we strive for perfection.

Your sanctification is within your own reach, and only you have control. What you put in is what comes out. Put in good seed, and you get good seed. Put in an evil word, and you get evil word. Watch what we hear, read, and even think, for each of these will infect the mind and speech.

List some good seed to grow on.

What did Jehoshaphat do in the time of trouble? Ask the people to cleanse themselves through a fast and begin to seek the Lord. I believe, if you had been there, you may have heard Jehoshaphat say, "Old God, cleanse us, forgive us, and hear us now from heaven."

Why? Jehoshaphat knew that before you could come before a holy

God, you must be cleansed of all sin. That is why sanctification is so important. To walk with your mind in control is to walk in peace with God and man. To have the mind of Christ is great and greatly pleases God. So when the time comes to call on God, we don't have to spend all our time asking the Lord to forgive us before we can ask him to help us. So, you see, what we feed our mind has a great impact on our life. We have to watch carefully what we read, hear, and see to live a victorious life in Christ Jesus.

Why is it so important for us to live a sanctified life? Explain. Why did Jehoshaphat tell the people to cleanse themselves? To walk with your mind in control is to walk in peace with God and man. Why?

Let's go back and look at ourselves a bit here and see what we have learned about ourselves.

1. What have you learned so far?
2. Did you see where you are in your walk with Christ?
3. Does looking inside your heart help you understand where you are now?
4. Has faith been increased by what you have learned currently in the book?
5. Has the power of positive thinking and speaking helped you draw closer?
6. Have you seen what the power of meditation means to you?
7. What is something we are to think about?
8. Describe what faith is.
9. Is faith a given thing?
10. If faith will grow, how will it?
11. All alone in a room, who is with you?
12. Can you see how to use the word of God in prayer?
13. How did Jehoshaphat pray?
14. Did Paul rejoice in tribulation?
15. Can you rejoice in tribulation?
16. List some life-changing moments.
17. Is there comfort in temptation? Explain.

18. Do you see the light at the end of the tunnel? Are you getting closer?
19. Who will never forsake you?
20. Explain what trust is.

These are twenty questions you need to ask yourself, and while doing so, be as honest as possible, knowing that spiritual growth is at stake here. While others may mock and laugh at your dedication, you can rejoice because you are going forward in faith, growing every day in Christ. It does not matter what the world thinks of you. God has the last word, so hold on and let him move you into a calling you could never dream of.

Chapter Ten

POWER OF POSITIVE SPEECH

What is the power of positive speech? Positive speech is the attitude of growth that comes from the heart. As we talk, people read us like a book, looking inside to discover what we are made of. Is it clear or fuzzy?

Positive speaking is not just a duty; it is a way of life. You live it, and then you will speak it. The ways of the Christian are not without adversity, but through the adversity, you will have to speak positive things.

Remember, the most powerful thing you can do for yourself is to speak positive things to yourself and about yourself. It is the window that controls your attitude and personality. The response of those words you speak determines what person you will be. It is not what happens to you, but what happens inside of you that controls the whole attitude of your being. Are we able to control our feelings, our emotions, or will we come back with a negative word of disbelief? It is natural to feel let down and cast out when things don't go our way, but speaking the right word over a situation is the greatest way to help yourself. The right word will carry you, and wrong words will hurt you. We must always speak the right words.

I want to mention some Bible verses that will help you achieve this goal of positive speaking. That is why I mention the power of positive thinking first because what we hear, see, and read governs the words that enter in the heart. Remember, Luke 6:45 says, "for of the abundance of the heart his mouth speaketh."

I want to tell you a story of my wife and me. My wife was one who always saw things at its worst. It did not matter what the situation was. Ninety percent of the time, she would speak some negative word about it. In 2001, I was sitting at the table while my wife was preparing supper. While she was preparing the table, she started talking about how bad things were and how God would never bring us out of this mess we were in. At that time, we were broke, just barely making ends meet. Our heads were just above the water.

As she was speaking, the Lord spoke to me and told me to get up and take her hand. I did not know what he would do, but I got up and said, "Let me see your hands."

She responded, "What? I don't know what you want. What are you going to do?"

I just said, "Let me see your hand." Then it came to me. As she took my hand, I said, "I want you to promise me that for the next ninety days, you will only speak positive things concerning our situation, and if God doesn't turn it around, I will never, ever say another word about you speaking negative again."

She did promise me she would do it. But for about three weeks, I had to say every now and then, "Remember what you promised me." She was about to start speaking those negative words again. Then she would remember and start saying positive things. And at the end of two whole months, she was only speaking those things that were positive to our situation.

All she needed was a little boost to get her out of that rut. Some of us need just a little boost from a spouse or friend to get us over the hump we are in. I urge you to find someone you can team up with and go for the positive talking, and you will be amazed at how much your life will change. But remember, you have to feed the mind with good words, encouraging words, for you to speak good words.

Can you change the way you think and speak? How do you change the way you think and speak?

As Christians, we have to learn that our Father and Lord Savior Jesus Christ are above all in you all and see your every need, whether a battle of the past or a battle at the moment. Philippians 4:6 says, "Be careful for nothing; but in everything by prayer and supplication with thanksgiving let your request be made know unto God." He wants to hear about it! It is his great desire to help us in every situation we have. So give him a chance and let him help you at this moment.

A place of refuge is a good place if it is used. In the Bible, cities were set aside just for places of refuge. Numbers 35:6 says, "And among the cities which ye shall give unto the Levites there shall be six cities for refuge, which ye shall appoint for the manslayer that he may flee thither."

Six cities were throughout the countryside: three cities east of the Jordan River designated to Moses and three cities west side of the Jordan River designated to Joshua, for the purpose of a house of refuge, for those who had committed murder, whether accidentally or unintentionally. Numbers 35:15 says, "These six cities shall be a refuge, both for the children of Israel, and for the sojourner among them; that every one that kill any person unaware may flee thither."

God made way for their provision, and he has made way for our provision to escape also. The house of refuge may be a church or a little mission ministry, regardless of where God has made provisions for you. The place of refuge is a dwelling for all to come to. But I want to make one quick comment, if I may. All churches are not a house of refuge. Some churches preach damnation, others preach condemnation, and a few just are not where they are supposed to be. Not understanding the word, some feel that your problems are brought on by you and only you. They feel that sickness is a sin you have committed, but listen to me. That is not correct. Had Job sinned when all the suffering came unto him? No!

Job 1:1 says, "There was a man in the land of Uz, whose name was Job; and that man was perfect and upright, and one that feared God, and eschewed evil." Does that sound like a man whose sin was why he lost all he had? No! Because you're having problems beyond your control and the pain of your past or the suffering you are living is at your door, this does not mean you have sin.

The house of refuge is there for all of us in the Lord, but we have to travel to it to get help. Look, the door will not open unless you open it. Revelation 3:20 says, "Behold I stand at the door and knock: if any hear my voice, and open the door, I will come in to him, and will sup with him, and he with me." As you see, you have to open the door first.

What are some of the provisions God has given unto us?

Help is only a heartbeat away, so find a house of refuge and some saint in the Lord that preaches or teaches the gospel and become an overcomer. The house of refuge can be a friend God has given special talents to or a person you trust dearly, but regardless of who it is, make sure they always edify you in the Lord. Remember, there's no value to the house of refuge when not in use; you have to go there. Only when you take advantage of such a place is when its value is of importance and means something.

The same goes for us when we don't take advantage of what God is willing to give us. It is like saying, "OK, God, I don't need you now. I can do it myself. I'll talk to you later." Each time this happens, we get farther and farther away from God, not realizing it. We find ourselves vulnerable and open to destruction.

Look, the house of refuge is still there, but you're not taking advantage of its uses, and by doing so, the house is not performing the duty it was designed to do.

God has put certain privileges and promises we can have in his great plan of salvation. If we fail to accept it, this does not mean the promises and privileges are gone, but you fail to receive the promises and privileges that were rightfully yours. The house of refuge is still there, just not performing its task as it was supposed to.

Chapter Eleven

BELIEVER MOTTO (PART TWO)

I mentioned the believer motto previously to show you what I do to help me grow in the Lord. But here you will get a deeper depth of the teaching from the passage the Lord gave me years ago.

The believer motto is a way of life. We will trust, obey, stand firm, and obey in all truth and shall not be moved. It's what we speak, what we do, and how we believe. As you read this article, let the words enter your spirit and build you up into a new way of thinking and speaking.

As Jehoshaphat held on to God's promises, so shall we hold to its promises also. Acts 10:34 says, "Then Peter opens his mouth, and said, of a truth I perceive that God is no respecter of person." We have the same privilege as the disciples did and others throughout history. So let's go and get our deliverances now, for God is no respecter of person.

The believer motto is a writing of certain scriptures that will help you build faith and strength to stand. We need to learn to meditate on it, and by meditating, I mean memorizing it until it is in you fully. We must hold on to God's word with all our strength and faith. Receive the word with all your might and strength. Call on the word with all your might and strength. John 1:1 says, "In the beginning was the word, and the word was with God, and the word was God." As you see the word, we can speak it is the word of God. That is why it is so powerful.

Mark 11:23 says, "For verily I say unto you, that whosoever shall say unto this mountain, be thou removed, and be thou cast into the sea; and shall not doubt in his heart, but shall believe that those things which he saith shall come to pass, he shall have whatsoever he saith." I will explain this verse later in this chapter.

Things I speak on a daily basis include the following:

- I can do all things in Christ Jesus.
- I will accomplish my goals.
- I am the righteousness of God.
- All blessing follows me.
- I have favor of the Lord.
- I have great health.
- Poverty is a thing of the past.

I have spoken it, so I will have faith, anointing, healing, finance, and spiritual gifts. I will not have doubt, poverty, shame, and unbelief.

I speak the following:

- These are mine.
- I have them by faith.
- I claim them now!

Why is this possible?   Because:

- My mind is made up according to his words that are in me.
- I feed the mind faith scripture, and I have faith.
- I feed my mind with positive beliefs, so I think positive belief.

Speak statements of truth daily and grow. Speak it and receive it as he has said. Learn it. Quote it. Stand on it. Memorize it. Hold on to it.

Chapter Twelve

THE STRENGTH OF THE WORD

One writer asks, "What does 'strength of the word' mean?" Is it to be smart? No! Is it to make people think you're great because you know a few scriptures? No! Well, why? The answer is here in Psalm 1:1–3, "Blessed is the man that walketh not in the counsel of the ungodly, nor standeth in the way of sinner, nor sitteth in the seat of the scornful. But his delight is in the law of the Lord; and his law doth he meditate day and night. And he shall be like a tree planted by the rivers of water, that bringeth forth his fruit in his season; his leaf shall not with; and whatsoever he doeth shall prosper)." Look at what the psalmist was saying.

What does holding on to God's word mean? When you speak, I am somebody. What are you really saying?

There are three areas the psalmist told us not to go:

1. Not in the counsel of the ungodly.
   Who are the ungodly, wicked, evil, and lacking reverence for God? Examples are deceit, lies, cursing, anger, and drunkenness.

2. Nor standeth in the way of sinners.
   The sinners are those lost without God, as we were. But they, for some reason, live to their fullness in the world, loving

worldly pleasure. He said, "Don't stand in the way; you are to help them, love them, and pray for them, but in no way are we to join them." If you stand in their way, they might pull you back into their lifestyle.

3. Nor sitteth in the seat of the scornful.
    The scornful mocked God, your salvation, and your beliefs. They have no part of that seat. Don't be drawn in by guile.

You may wonder why I am talking about this certain scripture when I really need help over past and present problems. Getting you to realize there is help and showing you how to receive help is a major hurdle to your healing.

You can go to every counselor in the world, but if you do not take heed to what he says, you still will not be healed. In this chapter, we talk about the book of Psalms, which is very rich with power, direction, and encouragement. Read it and meditate on things we can do. It is in our hands to do so.

Look at the scripture in Psalm 1:2–3 and see what it says.

First Part of the Scripture: "And he shall be like a tree planted by the rivers of water"

Notice this is his own condition. Before this can happen, you must first delight yourself in the law of God, love it, read it, desire it, and meditate upon it, day and night. And by doing so, you will be like a tree planted by the rivers of water. Look at the tall, green tree beside the river with deep roots. If we meditate upon the word, it is a river of nutrients that feeds us and causes us to grow in strength.

Second Part of the Scripture: "That bringeth forth his fruit in his season"

Notice, that same tree by the river will bear its fruit and it alone. A tree cannot bear the fruit of another, and neither can you. We each bear our fruit itself. I bear mine; you bear yours. But the amazing thing is, if we study and meditate upon the word, as he has said, we will bear our own fruit as God sees fit to give us.

THIRD PART OF THE SCRIPTURE: "HIS LEAF SHALL NOT WITHER"

Have you ever seen a thoroughly-watered tree die? No. And neither will you if you apply the water of the word.

FOURTH PART OF THE SCRIPTURE: "AND WHATSOEVER HE DOETH SHALL PROSPER"

When we apply these principles fully, the scripture will be fulfilled in us, "whatsoever he doeth shall prosper." But I am afraid we are living away from the privileges promised to us. The believer motto is a way to bring us back to where we need to be in God. It is a way to train our minds to meditate upon the Lord's word and feast on the river of life so we can grow in his grace. Now as we explore the believer motto, receive it and apply it, and you will grow in it.

Remember, you are somebody, and say it to yourself daily, "I am somebody. I am in good health. I am a good person." You see what I am talking about here. Say it and mean it.

Now faith is a funny thing. You can't buy it, you can't work for it, and you're not even born with it. It's the gift of God through his word. Some say, "Well, a baby knows there's a God. That has to be faith."

No, to know there is a God doesn't mean you have faith to trust in God, but to receive from God says you have faith. It's one thing to say you believe there's a God, but it's another to receive from God. You have to receive it, no matter what you ask for. I have seen people pray their hearts out with the power of God all over them. The anointing is so strong they couldn't contain it, and still they did not receive what they were seeking, whether it was healing, finance, or loved ones, all because they did not receive it. It is one thing to pray, and we must, but it is just as important to receive what you ask for. How do I do that?

1. Pray and ask God what you need first.
2. After you have prayed, say, "Lord, I receive that which I ask."
3. After you have received it, thank God for giving it to you.

Receive it, to have it, means what to you?

Your faith has come alive all because you have reacted upon it when you receive the word. How is that? When you pray, you say, "Lord, I believe it will come to pass." But without receiving it in you or upon the situation you pray about, I'm afraid you have been shortchanged. Faith is in you, isn't it? Yes. If you ask for something and don't receive it, you will not get it.

For example, say I want to borrow your car. You said okay, but I never received it to drive. I did not receive what I asked for. No. Why? If I had gotten the car I asked to borrow, I would have had what I had asked for. Is that not the same as receiving from God? You have to receive it before you get it. Ask for it and then receive it.

Romans 10:17 says, "So then faith cometh by hearing, and hearing by the word of God." Now that said a lot. Then what is faith? Faith only comes through the word of God. As you read the word of God with excitement and expectation, it just hides you in it. Along the way, you begin to see who Jesus really is. He becomes bigger than life to you. Jehoshaphat said in 2 Chronicles 20:7, "Art not thou our God, who didst drive out the inhabitants of this land before thy people Israel." Do you think Jehoshaphat would have prayed that type of prayer if he had no faith? No, he knew in whom he trusted. God was bigger than life to him, and he trusted him all the way.

So then what is faith, and how did Jehoshaphat get his faith to trust God?

Romans 10:17 says, "And hearing by the word of God, what has happened?" The word is speaking to you one on one. It is telling you things like, "It is yours, grab it … If he can have it, you can too … So-and-so was healed last week. You can be healed too."

"Try me," said the Lord. The whole time the word is speaking to you, you are moving mountains in your life. Why? The word is alive in you!

What faith is to you is a question you need to answer. Why? It might reveal how far away or close you are to the Lord. Some say they have faith, and another knows he has faith. What is the difference, my friend? One speaks from the heart; the other speaks from the mouth.

You may ask what the difference is. Some read and meditate on the word of God, along with fasting. Because of their dedication, faith has increased day by day, but others have done nothing but come to church and hear the word but never practiced what the word says. Just say their faith is weak. Faith cometh by hearing and hearing by the word of God. You have to put the word in you, and you have to trust him in all things, not just when you are in trouble. Once in a while, it is a lifestyle.

My wife and I preach in many churches, and to my amazement, I began to see that the faith to believe God can do anything was dead. They live right and all that, but the preacher did not preach on the power of God and what he could.

One morning in a Goldsboro, North Carolina, church, a mother came to me at the end of the service and asked if I would pray for her daughter to come back to church. She had not stepped foot in it in eighteen years. I called the congregation together and asked, "Do you believe in miracles?" And they said yes.

I said, "We are going to anoint a piece of cloth, and the mother will give it to her daughter. Tonight, her daughter will be sitting in this church."

You could see some look at one another and say to themselves, "Never heard this before." We prayed, and we went back that night to preach a sermon. When we pulled into the church parking lot, the mother ran to the car and said, "She's here! She's here! My daughter is here."

But look at what happened. Not only did she come herself, but she brought two more friends with her, and all three were saved that night. Why am I telling you this story? Our churches are dead in faith to believe that God can move one more time, but I know he can, and he will. Why did God allow me to speak such a word of faith that morning? Here is the reason: God will send someone from time to time to speak the word and do something out of the ordinary, like tell a crowd of one hundred saints of God that the mother and daughter would be in this church tonight without hesitations or unbelief.

Now I believe many came back that night just to see if the daughter did come back to see if I were what said would come to pass. Remember, I am no more than you are. I just believe what he says and what he tells me to do. Now did the devil fight me about what I had said with that prophecy? Yes! Always home and back to the church, I kept saying, "Devil, you are a liar. Get thee hence from me."

In a church in Jacksonville, North Carolina, I was preaching one Sunday morning, and in the middle of my sermon, the Lord stopped me and said, "Tell them I said, 'I am getting sick and tired of my children studying my word and knowing my word but not believing in my word.'"

You could have heard a pin drop to the floor. I finished preaching, and one old-timer approached me and said, "You hit it on the head of the nail."

I said, "The Lord did, and he means what he said. So now get this church to believing in the power of God again and watch it grow."

But I am telling you this so you can go to church every service and live as perfectly as a Christian is supposed to and still not see the power of God move. Why? I believe there are several reasons for that:

- The preacher does not have the message of the hour.
- The preacher may not be where he is supposed to be in Christ.
- The preacher may be out of his calling. He may be a teacher, pastor, or evangelist, but he has to be in what God called him for now. Or he may fulfill that position because God honors his word, but the preacher may need to get in the calling God has called him for to reap his full potential. This is my opinion and mine only. Many preachers and denominations have tried to tell me evangelists are of the past, but I would never give in to them because I know what I was called for, and it is an evangelist.
- It may be the church congregation. They may be in a divided state.
- Maybe you are not where you are supposed to be in the Lord.

No matter the reason, the power of God is not being manifested. It needs to be corrected.

Chapter Thirteen

SIX RULES OF GROWTH

Read it, digest it, consume it, live it, meditate on it, and receive it.

You can see the only way to receive from God is to give to God. Give yourself totally and completely. You will have to completely consume by his word and walk by his word. As we have already seen, to stand before God and pray a prayer like Jehoshaphat prayed, we first must know he will do it. Many come to the Lord and ask him for many things, but to much avail, nothing happens. Why is this? Maybe it's because we don't believe, or is it because we are not where we are supposed to be in the Lord? Only you can answer that question.

Now here we have a verse we are about to venture in, and it is deep. If you listen carefully to the spirit of the Lord, he will teach you how to receive once more again. I know you are wondering how this goes along with the power of positive thinking, the power of positive speech, and the prayer of desperation. Well, we are fixing to find out.

Look at this scenario for a moment. What do you think was happening when Jehoshaphat stood up in front of that crowd and prayed the prayer he prayed? Was it by hope he thought God might just hear him and answer his prayer, or was it because he knew that God would hear and answer him? What do you believe? He stood up in front of those people with no doubt that God would answer him. How do I know that? By the way he presented himself. Fearful, yes, but bold at the same time. You can be afraid of a situation and still have the boldness to stand before God and bring your petition for the situation.

Explain what fearful and boldness mean to you.

Look at Mark 11:23, "For verily I say unto you, that whosoever shall say unto this mountain, be thou removed, and be thou cast into the sea; and shall not doubt in his heart, but shall believe that those things which he saith shall come to pass, he shall have whatsoever he saith." What you think is very important and the way you speak is very important. Words are power, and words have authority. Jehoshaphat knew what to speak when oppressed by the enemy. Now let's see what happens when we hide the word of God in us. We become like Jehoshaphat because we know what to say.

1. He said that whosoever shall say to this mountain. That means anyone who has been born again can now speak to the situation, get its attention, let it know you are there. "Say, mountain, listen here …"
2. Now he said to tell the mountain what to do, "Be thou remove and cast into the sea." You spoke to it and got its attention. Now tell the mountain where to go. You now tell your situation what to do. You already have its attention. Now tell it what to do. Remember, it does not know what to do until you tell it. You've only got its attention. Tell it to be removed now and enter the place of destination, now the sea.
3. Now what if, "And shall not doubt in is heart." Faith is a four-letter word but packed with a lot of authority, authority to speak things into assistances or to speak things out of assistances like your mountain. But you cannot doubt, only believe.
4. And you, "But shall believe that those things which he <u>said</u> shall come to pass." Notice what the scripture is saying things that he said. (That is what you said.) Remember, you said it, so believe it.
5. Now, "He shall have what so ever ye saith." If you believe what you spoke and not doubt, you shall have what you spoke, but remember, you have to speak to the situation. The power is in

the faith. You have to believe God will do it for you, so let's take God at his word and start receiving some of the privileges we are supposed to have as Christians.

John 14:14 says, "If ye shall ask any thing in my name, I will do it." Again, here we see God is telling us to ask anything in his name, and he will do it. Notice the words *ask*. All miracles, whether they be big or small, are only granted through the name of Jesus, if you ask. But you must ask in faith. Not wavering is the key to you receiving your blessing.

You must train yourself to speak positively all the time and in every situation. To receive the answer, let the words of faith be so complete and full in you and your confidence that you know it is coming to pass.

What does it mean to get its attention when speaking to a mountain?

After praying for something, you cannot begin to ever doubt, and repeating things like "maybe he will do it" or "I hope he will" is tearing down your faith. This will bring in doubt, but in a settled way. It will slip in and over you, and you're not even aware of what has happened to your faith, all because of the wrong type of thinking and wrong speaking toward the prayer you prayed.

Many of us have problems we need to be healed from, but unless we believe, he will not do it. What we speak and think are very important, and we need to cherish it firmly. I know some of us have a lot of problems to deal with, and this is why I wrote this study manual. This manual is a guide to your clean living. We have to get our minds in focus on the word of God for us to think right and be able to receive from him.

Jehoshaphat was focused on the right thing. He was fully sure that God would do what he asked and deliver them from the enemy. 2 Chronicles 20:6 says, "And said O Lord God of our fathers, art not thou God in heaven? And rulest not thou over all the kingdom of the heathens? and in thine hand is there not power and might, so that none is able to withstand thee?" He said, "God, I know you are God in heaven, God over all the heathens with all power that none can withstand thee." Remember the paper I mentioned about the word *knowing*. Jehoshaphat knew God would do it. This is why he prayed such a prayer. We have to know as Jehoshaphat did.

Ecclesiastes 11:1 says, "Cast thy bread upon the water: for thou shall find it after many days." Here, we are told to cast our bread upon the water. What bread? Will we cast good bread that you eat upon the water to see it get soggy and dissolve? But we are going to cast our words upon the water. What are you saying? I am saying the words you speak are life and they are death.

Proverbs 18:21 says, "Death and life are in the power of the tongue: and they that love it shall eat the fruit thereof." The words you speak are either negative or positive or death and life. You want to cast the words upon the water so it can be nourished and carry on for another time. I believe the words we speak are bottled up in some way or another, so when we are hit with the worst of storms, the words we cast upon the water will come forth in the time of need. Matthew 7:12 says, "Judge not, that ye be not judged. For with what judgment ye judge, ye shall be judged: and with what measure ye mete, it shall be measure to you again."

How do you cast seed upon the water? Can you receive your words spoken back unto you again?

This is a very deep verse also, so let's investigate it now. Look at what he is saying. Judge not. What is this? I'm afraid we have been thinking that this means judge no one or you will be judged. Yes, it does, but it might be possible that the way you judge receiving the blessing of God could hinder you from receiving also. Why? If you in your mind says, "I wonder if it will come to pass," you have judged it by saying "without full faith." And doing so will cause the judgment you spoke upon that situation to return to you and without measure.

In other words, the doubt has come back to you, but this time without measure. Each time we speak upon a thing, it does not matter what it is. The word will come back to us, some to faith and others to doubt. If you have spoken the words of doom over your situation, what we are going to receive is the words of doom.

Words have power. The old saying, "sticks and stones can hurt my bones, but words can never harm me," is so far from the truth, and it is pathetic. It's one of the biggest lies Satan has ever put on a Christian. Words build up, and words tear down. James 1:10 says, "Out of the same mouth proceedeth blessing and cursing. My brethren, these things ought not so to be." See, the power is within us. Whether we bless or curse with our words, it is ours. 2 Corinthians 9:10 says, "Now he that ministered seed to the sower both minister bread for your food, and multiply your seed sown, and increase the fruits of your righteousness."

What is he saying? You were given seeds to sow, "seeds of God's words." As you speak the word, you have sowed it. It becomes food of strength, the bread of life, and it feeds you. The words sown are multiplied because you have sown them, and the fruits of your righteousness have been increased because you sowed the seed given you.

Let me put this in commonsense terms. You spoke the word you receive, and it was multiplied because you spoke it, and that was accounted for in the increase in your fruits of righteousness. Remember Matthew 7:1–2 about how words return to us. If we judge negative, we reap negative; if we judge positive, we reap positive. Matthew 7:12 says, "Judge not, that ye be not judged. For with what judgment ye judge, ye shall be judged: and with what measure ye mete, it shall be measure to you again)." Also look at Proverbs 16:24, "Pleasant words are as honeycomb, sweet to the soul, and health to the bones."

Positive word is the turning of intention into reality, in which the words spoken were fitted for the occasion. Negative words are never fitted for the occasion only to be destroyed, so learn to speak words of life and strength. Faith can be destroyed, and faith can be built up. The task is up to us. Jehoshaphat spoke the word of life to frightened people. Even Jehoshaphat was fearful, but not in the sense he could not think for himself. It was then when the pleasant words of the honeycomb came unto the hearer. Life is the inner core of your being. Lose hope and see how you feel; get hope and see how you feel. There's as much difference as day and night. The word of life, like the words of a honeycomb, was the food to the faith. When faith is down, you are down, but let faith be alive and see the quest you can conquer.

Jehoshaphat brought life through the word of a honeycomb when he stood in front of the congregation and prayed and said, "Let's call a fast."

This was as sweetness to the soul and health to the bones to those that were in fear. The glory of winning comes alive through the nourished honeycomb of life.

Listen, "A word fitly spoken is like apples of gold in picture of silver" (Proverbs 25:11). Here's what Solomon is saying, "Think for a moment about a great happening that has happened in your life, something disturbing to the point it alarms you, how that someone said something to you out of the way, and the words they said did not really set with you." Then a friend heard it and said what he was trying to say was not what it sounded like he did not mean to say it like that. And this seemed to pacify you to the point that you soon got over it.

This is what Solomon is talking about in Proverbs 25:11. He is saying that sometimes words are spoken in a picture of silver, which does not have the value of gold and does not hold the same value either. But when the word of gold is added to the picture of silver, it gives it a completely different meaning. Do you get the picture of a word fitly spoken and words as a honeycomb, how they are the lifeline of what we are? Will people see us as pictures of silver only, or will they see a picture of gold with the words cometh forth as pleasant words of honeycomb? The choice is up to us.

Are you what you speak? Explain how that can be. Do your words reveal who you are? Think on that and answer. Explain the term *honeycomb* in Proverbs 16:24. Explain how the picture of silver and gold has related to some of your circumstances. Can you speak the word of a honeycomb to them that has just offended you, and can you put the gold of life upon the silver picture?

We will discuss the area a little further in this book about what to think on and what to speak.

Remember, faith comes through the word of God and only through the word. Reading and listening to the word of God is the only way to receive faith. You were given a measure of faith from the beginning, but it's not enough to sustain you for the long haul. You have to study the word of God daily, no ifs, ands, or buts about it, to have great faith. Also ask the Lord to increase your faith. Romans 10:17 says, "So then faith cometh by hearing and hearing by the word of God."

I was sitting in my rocking chair, meditating upon the Lord when I asked him to show me what faith is. As I was sitting there, I looked at my refrigerator door. As I looked, I saw the number from the bottom to the top of the door. The number started with zero as a measure of faith. Then it went up the door from number one to number ten, the largest. He told me zero is the measure of faith that everyone gets from accepting the Lord Jesus Christ as their Savior. All the rest are given to you as you increase in faith through reading the word, overcoming trials, trusting God with your issues, prayer life, fasting, and dedication. Faith is fair to all. You earn it!

Note: The baptisms of the Holy Ghost give you a gift of faith. It is one of the nine gifts in 2 Corinthians 12:8–11. But you must be filled with the baptisms of the Holy Ghost with the evidence of speaking in tongues or as the spirit gives utterance stated in Acts 2:1–4. Look them up and please read.

How does the word of faith increase in you? Explain two areas.

The Lord has given us the anointing when we receive the spirit of God. The anointing will teach you to pray and guide you into all truth and is no lie. It will open up the word of God to you like you have never seen before and add to your faith daily. It is the anointing we so desperately need in our lives. Pray daily, saying, "I have the anointing of God in me." 1 John 2:27 says, "But the anointing which ye receive of him abideth in you, and ye need not that any man teach you, but as the same anointing teacheth you of all things, and is no lie, even as it hath taught you, ye shall abide in him."

He said he would teach you himself; all we have to do is let him. Look at Isaiah 45:3, "I will give thee hidden riches of secret places." Isaiah said there are hidden treasures you cannot even see: treasures of healing, treasures of good health, treasures of blessed children, treasures of comfort, treasures of peace, and treasures of riches, which there is no end to. John said he wished above all that they may prospered as thy soul prospered. Look what he said, "as thy soul prospered." It is God will's that we all prosper, but to prosper as our soul prospered in the Lord. 3

John 2 says, "Beloved, I wish above all thing that thou mayest prosper and be in health even as thy soul prospered."

Look, there is nothing wrong with wanting money, but when that's all we can think about then, we have a serious problem. To prosper in our health and soul is the greatest prospering of all; all the others will be added in their due season. But remember, learning how to talk and speak is very vital to our receiving from God. It is the courses of direction in which we must train ourselves to walk in. It goes back to the power of positive speech and the power of positive thinking. It becomes a way of life. You walk it, think it, and talk it without even being aware of it, but you have to train yourself to do so. It's not easy, but you can do it. Old tricks are sometimes hard to break, but you will succeed. It is the training of oneself to always talk positively.

Here is the key! Speak to yourself, saying, "I am somebody. I have the blessing of God! Blessings will follow me all the days of my life. I can move mountains!" You have to train yourself to live positively through every situation, looking on the bright side of the issue.

God is waiting on us. It's not us waiting on God, for he is always ready to bless. Psalm 91:15 says, "He called upon me and I will answer him: I will be with him in trouble: I will deliver him, and honor him." This is a promise, so let's call upon him now.

To find hidden treasure is to do what? List at least three areas in your life and in Jehoshaphat's life also.

Now, I want to discuss nine areas Paul speaks about in Philippians 4:8, "Finally, brethren, whatsoever things are true, whatsoever things are honest, whatsoever things are just, whatsoever things are pure, whatsoever things are lovely, whatsoever things are of good report; if there be any virtue, and there be any praise, think on these things."

Now we have gotten to one of the most important verses, I believe, in this book because this is where we find out what we are to think on and what to speak. We need to know this because, if we don't, we will find ourselves not learning anything. And not learning what to think and speak will cause us to go on in our own way, as was before.

This book intends to help us out of the old way of negativity and go on into virtuous things. So here we are. Oh, by the way, do you think Jehoshaphat had a positive attitude toward the situation when the army was encamped about them, and do you think the lesson learned from Jehoshaphat is a lesson of leadership? Was Jehoshaphat a leader and a servant? I will explain. He was a leader in the sense that he stood up to what he had to do, and that was called on God to relieve the fear of his people. Doing so made him a great steward of his own people and steward of God by trusting that God would fight his battle for him.

Explain a good steward. Explain what loyalty is. Who should loyalty be to?

Let's go a little deeper now to where we are. 1 John 1:14–15 says, "and this is this confidence that we have in him, that, if we ask anything according to his will, he hears us. And if we know that he hears us, whatsoever we ask, we know that we have the petition that we desired of him." What is Peter saying here? Let's go and dissect it now.

1. **"and this is this confidence that we have in him"**: You have to trust and know he will do what his word has said. If not, you will not receive.
2. **"that, if we ask anything according to his will, he hears us"**: Yes, again, you have to know that the word in the Bible is true and it is God's word he is speaking. He cannot lie, and what he says will come to pass.
3. **"And if we know that he hears us, whatsoever we ask, we know that we have the petition that we desired of him"**: Now this is deep. We know he hears us. Whatsoever we ask of him, we know we receive the answered prayer we ask about. Why? We believe in his word, not man or beast, but the word of God. And because of that, we know it is his own way, no questions asked. There are a lot of prayers I have seen come to pass, and there are some that have not yet. Well, now why is that? Notice, I said some that have not come to pass. Because I know they are coming, but in his time, or maybe it is because we are not in the area or place he wants us yet. Maybe we were supposed to turn

right, and we turned left. So God has to get you back on course, and sometimes it is a long way around to the other side of the hill when we should have gone across the top of him. Either way, most of the time, if the prayer has not come yet, there's a little something wrong, and only you can figure out what went wrong and what you need to do to get back on track. So let's look at our life and see if we missed it somewhere along the way. I bet we have. I have made the wrong turn many times, and it took several years to get me back where he wanted me, to my shame. I did not understand what he was telling me, and sometimes I'm just stubborn.

Chapter Fourteen

BIRTH IN HAVING FAITH

Now as I explain all nine parts of the verse mentioned previously, I want you to take a look at yourself and see if you are where you are supposed to be in the Lord.

Philippians 4:8 says, "Finally, brethren, whatsoever things are true, whatsoever things are honest, whatsoever things are just, whatsoever things are pure, whatsoever things are lovely, whatsoever things are of good report; if there be any virtue, and there be any praise, think on these things."

"Whatsoever thing are true"

What are true? Is it wealth, fame, or success? I will say not! Whatsoever things that are true or shall, I say whatsoever things that are truth. They are the ingredients of your own making and within your own soul. It's what you are. Riches can be truth, for it only reveals possession. Fame can't be true or truth because it only brings forth glamour. Success can't be, for all is vanity, as Solomon says. Ecclesiastes 2:11 says, "Then I look on all my works that my hands had wrought, and on the labor that I labor. To do: and behold, all was vanity and vexation of the spirit, and there wan no profit under the sun." Here, we are being told to be honest with ourselves and others. Solomon has said all I achieve in life was but vanity.

As you can see, all that is anything but true or truth is vanity. But what, my friend, is true or truth? True or truth, as I may have the permission to say so, is being true to you or maybe truth about yourself. Do you really know you, or are you living in a fairy tale? To grow in the Lord is to become like a person under an x-ray machine, with nothing hidden before the Lord. Now we know that the Lord knows all things already, but he wants us to tell him about it, like talking to your big brother or sister. In other words, he wants you to carry your littlest to your biggest secrets of weakness to him.

Many times, we, as people of God, have put ourselves down. We belittle ourselves to the point that we feel as if we are nobody. I'm telling you that you are somebody. Maybe you do have some problems, but who doesn't? We've all been to a place where we felt like we were a nobody. But always be true to yourself and others. In other words, believe in you.

We are vulnerable to hurt and pain that digs deep into our souls. And sometimes we are not the blame for this hurt inside. This hurt can come from the closest of friends or a loved one, and when it does, it is like a stronghold that enters into the deepest of the heart and mind working to destroy. But 2 Corinthians 10:4–5 says, "For the weapons of our warfare are not carnal, but mightily through God to the pulling down of strong holds" (casting down imagination and every high thing that exalted itself against the knowledge of God and bringing into captivity every thought to the obedience of Christ). The spirit of Christ has been sent to tear down this stronghold trying to destroy us.

The weapons of obedience and faith in the Lord tear down the stronghold in our life. But we have to be honest with ourselves in everything. Faith is one of the greatest things to be dishonest about. They say they believe God will bring them out with one voice, and the next voice says, "I hope God will do it for me." My friend, it is his will to give unto you the best of his blessing. 3 John 2 says, "Beloved, I wish above all thing that thou mayest prosper and be in health even as thy soul prospered." You see, he wants you to be blessed, so now be blessed. You are the one who is in control of that. You were given the keys of the kingdom, so now unlock the wonderful blessing of God and live a victorious life.

Matthew 18:19 says, "And I will give unto thee the keys of the kingdom of heaven: and whatsoever thou shall bind on earth shall be bound inn heaven: and whatsoever thou shall loose on earth shall be loosed inn heaven." Do you see what he is saying? The work is up to you and you only. The Lord has done all he will do, so now let's start to work. Lose the hold in your life, and live and bind it up and cast it out of your way and receive the blessing of our Lord and Savior.

If you are not truthful over the small things, how can you be truthful over the big things? When we say we have faith and doubt, we lie against the truth. The truth in you is all that will prevail in troubled times. Time is the killer in most of us because we have put off what we know is our problem from the beginning. If we are weak, let's say to the Lord we are weak and need help. Then truth is turned to truth as a river of life in your blood. Proverbs 16:24 says, "Pleasant words are as a honeycomb, sweet to the soul, and health to the bones." Pleasant words are words of truth and power, so let's speak truth in all we do.

Trouble will come, and trouble will go, but you are still here. You are stronger than you thought you were. Tests and trials are for but a moment, but truth is forever. He said he would bring you out of the situation you are in. Just believe him. Speak the word of truth, and be truthful with yourself and God. If you are weak in an area, say you are weak. Don't play the big man in town. Be yourself and nobody else. I am weak in some areas, but I am asking the Lord to help me all the time. But watch here for a moment. As you ask him to help you, he also wants you to help yourself. Do that which is in your power to do.

Look here a moment? The book's title is *Prayer of Desperation*, and the section's title is "whatsoever things are true." You may be wondering how both titles are to come together. Look at this thought for a moment. When in distress, as was Jehoshaphat, he kept his right spirit because he was truthful to God and himself. He knew where he was at with God and did not have to worry about what no one would say. Truthfulness is the food that will feed the soul and the spirit. "The devils also believed and tremble" (James 2:19). Why? He could not accept the truth. God only accepts truth and faith.

God could not accept the devil because he knew he was not true. He was living a lie. I wonder if that's some of our problems with receiving from the Lord Jesus Christ. Are we what we are, or are we living a lie?

To be true is to be true. Well, that is defined well, I may say. Why? Being true overrides the spirit of discouragement, but being true is the sense of belief in oneself, to know he will answer when you call upon him. It is the lifeline of one's faith and love that draws the inner working of man to the point of surrendering to God totally. Proverbs 10:12 says, "Hatred stirreth up strifes: But love covereth all sins."

In other words, the true part of you comes from God. We are all born with a sinful nature, and if any good thing comes out of us, it is due to the true fullness we are in our Lord Jesus Christ. That's why Solomon could say, "Love covereth all sin" and James 5:20 says, "Let him know, that he which converteth the sinner from his way shall save a soul from death and hide a multitude of sins."

When we are true to the sinner or saint of God, we become a picture of gold, not a picture of silver we discussed previously. Our true or truth is the ship from which we can get in to carry us forward, but people will not understand you at times either and begin to doubt you but know you are truth. It is the area where people judge you, whether you are truth or lie. It is the key to what we are in all our works. To be true is to be true in mind, words, deeds, trust, loyalty, stewardship, and love. As I may say, be true to you, others, and God always.

"WHATSOEVER THINGS ARE HONEST"

I believe things that are true and the things that are honest are closely related, with some minor differences in their calling. What do I mean? We are called to live honestly before God and man and to be honest with ourselves. Honest is the given full worth of value, not a cheater, liar, or thief, but honest to others as well as yourself, always speaking the truth. Honest and true are related. To know you is to know truth. But to hide truth and honest is deception to you and others. Search the inward part of the heart and mind and see if you are honest with yourself. The inward part of man is in constant battle with himself. The battle of the mind and warfare of the spirit is an ongoing process every day.

So now whatsoever things are honest, what is it? It is the thinking on those things that are truth and not a lie. Well, what are some things that are honest to think on? Now let's look at ourselves for a moment and see what we can see. What do you see? Do you see the part of you that brings forth honesty? Do you see the part of you that sees love? Can you see the part of you that is of good deeds?

I say all those have their rightful place in our lives, but it's not what Paul was talking about here. Paul is basically saying, "Think on things that are of God and of pleasant moments." As it is with "whatsoever things are true," the same holds true with both. Think on things that are of value and will bring consolation to us, whether through the word or by something that has happened in your life.

Make sure what you think on is of value. It is a great thing to think about where God has brought us, but watch dwelling on things that have brought pain to your lives. I have at times dwelled on the things that are good, and then in a moment, I find myself dwelling on those pains of the past. And to my amazement, I find it a lot harder to get my mind back on the things of value than it was to fall into the things of doom. But hold on and try to get your focus back as quickly as possible.

Also, there is another area of this, "whatsoever things are honest," we need to discuss. Look, sometimes you are trying to blame someone else for something you know you're just hanging on to. Maybe it just feels good knowing you can hang on to it. Or just maybe there is nothing to it, but you are hanging on to it because it makes you feel good. You will have to decide that for yourself. But I'm telling you from experience that it will come back and get you before it gets the other person. The best thing for you is what Paul said in Philippians 4:8, "think on these things." What? These are the things that are true and honest. All the others are but dung. Learn that scripture by heart, meditate upon it, hold to it, let it, and guide your mind into great and pleasant things in the Lord.

Note: Be aware of your honesty and watch what you may tell. This subject is talking about your honesty and truth fullness to yourself and God. In other words, are you where you are supposed to be in the Lord? Have you made others feel you are this great giant of a man or a woman who can move great mountains? Truthfulness and honesty in the Lord is the key. Remember, the Lord already knows what you are anyway. If you are hurting inside, tell him; if you need help over a thing, tell him.

Be honest and let's grow. You would be surprised about the person who says everything is all right in their life when you can see the pain on their face. But pride and ego will not let them see the truth. So let's be truthful and get the help we need and live.

Also we are talking about being true and honest in the sense of thinking on that which is true and honest. What are some things that are true and honest? Well, let's see here for a moment. You are somebody. You are a chosen vessel. You are a royal priesthood. You are a servant of the highest God. As you can see, there is a lot. We can think on that is true and honest. Just say, "I am somebody," and tell the Lord, "I am of the highest God. His royal priesthood has clothed me, and I am in him, and he is in me." Speak on those and rejoice on it and say, "Lord of Hosts, you're my God now. I will have a clear mind dwelling on things of virtue, receive the things of value, and be blessed in all my going, said the Lord of Hosts, my Lord and my Savior Jesus Christ. My Lord, this I will receive because I have received."

Why is it so important to always be honest and true with yourself? List some reasons why we are to think on positive things. List seven things we need to receive from the Lord.

"Whatsoever things that are just"

This is defined as just is the act of fair with impartial just. It is the judgment of truth in our Christian walk. It will judge you in all your deeds and hold you accountable of all, and if found worthy, it will place the value of the blessed word just upon your name.

So to be just is to be fair to yourself. Also, to be just is also being fair to others. So then fair is the act of you being just. So then being just is the key of being just. It is the moral of a man or woman. It has no other verdicts. It is plain and simply nothing taken or added, only being what God planned for it to be. But I fear that most of us don't even know what being just is and have never thought about it either. Why do you suppose that? We don't see it as a great issue. But as you read this, you will see it is a great issue and needs to be dealt with very seriously. Why?

To your amazement, just is a virtuous word, meaning a virtuous person or a just person spoken in the light of moral issues. Acts 10:22 says, "And they said, Cornelius the centurion, a (JUST) man, and one that feareth God." Matthew 1:19 reads, "Then Joseph her husband, being a (JUST) man, and not willing to make her publick example, was minded to put her away privily." Proverbs 24:16 states, "For a (JUST) man falleth seven times, and riseth up again: but the wicked shall fall into mischief."

As you can see, the word *just* holds a place of value spoken in the right content. So what does "whatsoever things are just" mean? It is the inner part of a man or woman that does righteously.

Here we are talking about things to think on as well as just men the Bible speaks about. But why are they called just men? Look at Joseph for a moment. When he found out Mary, his wife-to-be, was with child, he thought to dispose of her privately, to keep anyone from hearing about it, and destroy her name. But as he thought on that, an angel appeared to him and told him not to, but to take her and go unto her, for the child was God's child and he was to name him Jesus. As you can see here, Joseph was willing to do the right thing.

You can see what a just man is. He is willing to do that which is morally right, no matter the situation. But that still does not answer the question concerning "whatsoever things are just," does it? What kind of and statement is this? In one sense, we have been talking about a just person and what character they possess. But on the other hand, we have not spoken of the types of things we are to think on.

To be just is to be what in Christ?

What are some of the things we are to think on? What would they be? Now we find ourselves looking back into the area we have already discussed to find out how much it all ties together. Just look at how they all run in parallel to one another.

To think on a just thing is like thinking on that which is pure, and to think on that which is pure is like thinking on that which is honest, and all three are the way of the honeycomb or the way of gold picture on a silver picture. Why? You cannot think on just honest things and not have pure things involved with your thinking, and neither can you think on just things alone without drawing from that which is pure or honest. You cannot have one without drawing from the other.

That's not to say that all three of those, "whatsoever things are true," "whatsoever things are honest," and "whatsoever things are just," want to be in this area to themselves because they will. It has its own area of power, which are those things to think on. One will be in this order, and the other will be in that order, but they will never be in conflict with one another. They will all work hand in hand together, bringing both comforts in words and in truth within oneself. It is the lifeline of your inner being or strength to stand in perilous times.

You may say you still have not told me what to think on as far as whatsoever things are just. This, my friend, looks to be a hard one to answer, but it is the easiest one to answer. Why? To think justly is to judge rightfully. Remember, Matthew 7:1–2 says, "Judge not, that ye be not judge. For with what judgment ye judge, and with what measure ye mete, it shall be measure to you again." When we think only on the things of value and virtue, we have not the time to judge another based on what we may see or hear. When we are letting the justly act of just thinking take over our thought and our words, we find ourselves thinking on things that are pure and honest as well.

So then, to think on just things is something like looking into a mirror and saying, "All is good around me, I hear nothing, and I think nothing. I only see me and my walk with Jesus, not the garbage of past or present. I see Jesus and all the needs of the people, but I do not take thoughts of the past or present or things that will beset me."

I am sorry, but we have to venture into an area of that verse, "whatsoever thing are just," and discuss the side most of us are walking in the side of judgment and self-pity, knowing all the time we've made ourselves look as if we are doing fine when the reality is we're not. We are lost inside, only to hide the feeling that has bugged us for ages. We are not willing to admit we have a problem, and we are going on as if everything is okay the whole time, lying to ourselves and others.

A just mind is a place where peace and comfort dwell and confidence has dominion. When the mind is in a mess, we are in a mess. Let's not lie to ourselves, but let's be true, honest, and just, no matter what. If we need help, don't be afraid to get it. God is waiting for you to call on him.

Your brother and sister in the Lord are waiting for you to call on them, so let's do the right thing, to get help and go forth to victory.

But we have the habit of lying to ourselves and trying to make others think we have no problem when we do. Just like truth, honest, and just are all similar in ways, it still takes all three working together for us to be complete. Look in the mirror and see who you see and who you might surprise. You might see in the mirror who is lying to himself and realizing he is his worst enemy. Or you might see in the mirror the real person inside.

A just spirit is as pleasant as the honeycomb or the gold that covers the silver on the picture. It is as glamorous and bright as the noonday. But to hide ourselves in the daily trouble of affairs and not on the things of truth or honesty with a just spirit is a disaster of great magnitude.

To think in a just attitude is to dwell on things of honesty and truth, or as the scripture has stated, true and honest, and this walk of completion. It is the walk of moral conduct with the right spirit of true and honest in its daily affairs. All is great and well with your soul, for you know that as the pillar of cloud by day and the fire by night, which led the children of Israel, so will your God lead you by his word. For the word of truth with an honest and just spirit are as lamps unto your path of growth. It is part of the light that will shine upon your walk in the Lord. So learn to walk in honest, truth, and just spirit with your heart, soul, and mind, thinking on things of virtue and value and growing in the Lord.

"WHATSOEVER THINGS ARE PURE"

To be pure is to be free from anything. That damages you from walking in the presence of others as well as with yourself. It is the calling of oneself to walk holy, free from sin. This also covers the area of seeing, hearing, and speaking things contrary to the word of God. In other words, it means walking in a state of pure holiness all the time.

Now to be pure is to be holy, isn't it? To be pure is to be presentable to God and man, isn't it? Well, it is the walking of holy conviction and loyalty to God and man, bringing the spirit man into a place in God where you dwell in holy things. You think holy, talk holy, and act holy, for it is the lifeblood of your being.

The pureness of oneself tells you what about him?

Then what is this, "whatsoever things are pure"? What is this? It's the area we must think on, I might add. It is the pureness of thought! It's the power of one's speech and the character one portrays. It's the action of one's stewardship one must show. It is also the state of one's being in which one walks; it's the total consecration of himself to be Christ-like.

It's the motion of pureness in heart and mind. It's the training of one's thought and lifestyle. It's the moving of the wheel into a state of control and guidance through the discipline of one's self-will.

You and only will govern yourself. The Lord will never go against your will, if you do not want to. It is a sovereign thing unto the Lord. Your calling is of him and must be accepted with your desire to serve, no matter what you are asked to do.

There are some things in all our lives that we all wish could go away, but to our amazement, we find it pops its ugly head back up from time to time. You see, we all have a problem trying to live a lifestyle of thinking upon things that are true, honest, just, and now pure.

But I realize most of us are still fighting a battle in the mind. I just want to say that we will always have a battle in the mind to fight. Satan is going to try to throw everything he possibly can at you.

The mind is a place where Satan hits the hardest. It is the past in our lives he mostly uses against us. Why? Ephesians 6:12 says, "For we wrestle not against flesh and blood, but, against principalities, against powers, against the rulers of darkness of this world, against spiritual wickedness in high places."

We are in constant warfare with these principalities, powers, and rulers of darkness. They are spirits of Satan sent to destroy mankind. They never tire and never give up, always seeking to destroy you. The devil is a roaring lion. John 10:10 says, "The thief cometh not, but for to steal, and to kill, and to destroy I am come that might they have life, and that they might have it more abundantly." The devil has come to destroy us, but we have power over him in the name of Jesus.

Matthew 16:19 says,

> And I will give unto you thee keys of the kingdom of heaven: and whatsoever thou shalt bind on earth shall be bound in heaven: and whatsoever thou shalt loose on earth shalt be loosed in heaven.) Look we have the power to bind Satan and put him where he belongs by the name of Jesus. He said whatsoever you BIND or LOOSE on earth is in agreement with heaven that, what you said shall come to pass." Isaiah 5:11 reads, "So shall my word be that goeth forth out of my mouth: it shall not return unto me void, but it shall accomplish that which I please, and it shall prosper in the thing whereto I sent it.

Notice what he is saying. What we speak shall not return to you and say, "I can't do that," but it will do what you say if you believe. It shall accomplish that which you spoke.

Learning how to fight the devil with a pure word of comfort and not of shame is a very vital source of comfort to know, for it is his word we fight with. Jehoshaphat knew what he would speak before the congregation. He knew God would back up the word he would speak to the children of Israel.

Did Jehoshaphat have the spirit of the servant? If yes, explain.

Dwell on those things that are of truth that will bring forth a pure conscience, not slow full in duty, but one who desires to grow in grace. Dwell in the presence of holy things and hear only holy words, and as the writer has said, think on those things. For it shall be unto you as a "pleasant words are as an honeycomb, sweet to the soul, and health to the bones" (Proverbs 16:24). The words you dwell on are very important in your spiritual walk into the Lord.

What we dwell on and what we surround ourselves with has a great impact over our life. This motion keeps you in the motion of blessing or discouragement. There's no greater joy to have than knowing we have walked in the presence of the Lord, knowing he hears and answers our prayer when we call on him.

When Jehoshaphat called upon the Lord, he did two very relevant things, I believe. He caused the people of Judah to trust in the Lord our God, and it showed the people of Judah he was still in charge.

Sometimes in life, we have to stand up against the enemies. We have to stand strong in times of conflict. But when we are in a mess ourselves, we are not good for anything except to belly-ache. That is why we have to learn how to keep ourselves in the right way for God. The mind will carry you from being strong in the Lord one moment to a panicked state the next. God wishes that we all never panic under pressure, but I am afraid we do. Remember what Paul has been saying here so far in Philippians 4:8, "Finally, brethren, whatsoever things are true, whatsoever things are honest, whatsoever things are just, whatsoever things are pure, whatsoever things are lovely, whatsoever things are of good report; if there be any virtue, and there be any praise, think on these things."

He is saying to us, "Think on these things, and in the hard times, you will be able to stand." As you know, Jehoshaphat feared, but it did not deter him from standing against the enemy. He was anchored in on what he knew, what he had seen, and what he had heard his forefather talk about. We have to turn back to this if we will ever see the Lord move miraculously again, standing for what is right, no matter what, if all alone. Jehoshaphat knew it was not right for the enemy to come and try to take his Promised Land, so he stood against them, and it brought an establishment of people who some probably had never seen the Lord work a miracle among them before. We must stand as Jehoshaphat did and turn a whole country around by God's word and power.

Now we will venture into another area of Philippians 4:8, which covers areas such as "whatsoever things are lovely, whatsoever things are of good report; if there be any virtue, and there be any praise, think on these things."

We will start with "whatsoever things are lovely" and "whatsoever things are of good report." I put both together because I think they are related to each other. As it was with "whatsoever thing are true/honest/just/and pure" work together, so do these. Each one is of itself and in need of the other as well. As one hand washes the other, so will each one correspond with the other.

"WHATSOEVER THINGS ARE LOVELY, WHATSOEVER THINGS ARE OF GOOD REPORT; IF THERE BE ANY VIRTUE, AND THERE BE ANY PRAISE, THINK ON THESE THINGS) IS THE REJOICING OVER GOOD TIME, THE HAPPINESS IN OTHER SUCCESS, WITH THE JOY OF LOVE IN YOUR HEART"

What then is "whatsoever things are lovely and whatsoever things are of good report it if there be any virtue, and if there be any praise"? It is the bringing of oneself into a place of praise for the other. It is the bringing of oneself into a position to rejoice while the other is being blessed.

What are we to think on? It is the dwelling of good deeds done to others as well as to ourselves. It is the rejoicing in good and bad times. The will to rejoice while others are being blessed is one most people have a problem with. They say they are happy for you, but you can feel they are not. The sign of turnoff and rejection are relevant in their speech and action.

Explain what virtue and praise are together.

This happens a lot among Christians, my brother and sister, and this should not be. That is why Paul was saying here, "think on things that are lovely and of a good report, and if any praise or any virtue think on those things." Why was that? When you have the right mindset, things do not bother you quite as badly. To have praise of others on your mind rather than having what you have accomplished on your mind is the first step to growth in humility. Matthew 23:12 says, "And whosoever shall exalt himself shall be abased; and he that shall humble himself shall be exalted."

To lift oneself up in his own glory is to be shamed in his own glory, for there will be no one there to glory with him, for his glory has come to shame.

What am I trying to say? When we are lifted so high that we cannot

97

see other people's blessing, only our own, we have just lost the battle to our mind. Why? You cannot glory in other men's blessing unless it's the blessing of good reports and the blessing of lovely praises. There's no way you can rejoice in another man's blessing if the blessing of peace is not operating in you. If you don't think so, try it. Just quit thinking on the things of good value and see what happens the next time someone begins to tell you of a great big blessing God has done for them. If you want to have to fight yourself, rejoice with them. Why? The rejoicing spirit of praise and virtue is not in action.

In other words, he is saying you did not have your mind on the thing that brought praise and virtue to you. He said, "Think on things that are lovely and things that are of good report." Why? It brings oneself under control, being obedient to the spirit of God.

The greatest hope of our strength among one another is when we rejoice over the blessing they have received and not ours only. It's one of the greatest wheels that have ever been to jump-start and relationship with. When we rejoice with one another, it is one of the keys to unlocking the spirit of despair.

Rejoice in one another, and rejoice gladly. Receive the glory of life, which is comfort in one another. I hope you have learned how important it is to walk in the spirit. It is not a hard task but a steadfast task, bringing oneself under submission to the word of God. All through this book, I have tried to make it plain so a child in the Lord could understand it. I hope I have succeeded in doing that. May God bless you and be with you in all your study.

Chapter Fifteen

A QUIZ TO CHECK YOURSELF

The following are questions you can go back and find the answers to.

1. Did you catch how Jehoshaphat prayed that prayer when faced with a terrible situation? Would you have prayed that way if you were faced with the same situation? Was that a proper way to pray?
2. When in a fight of your mind, is it proper to use the power of positive thinking? Explain that in your way.
3. Was Jehoshaphat a leader? And if so, explain what he did to make you think he was.
4. What is prayer of faith to you, and what was it to Jehoshaphat? Explain each one individually.
5. Explain the difference between the power of positive thinking and the power of positive speech. How do they apply to you and Jehoshaphat? How are they applied?
6. Do you see what Jesus meant when he said, "love your enemies"? Explain how that is possible. Give at least three answers.
7. Is the broken heart or a broken spirit mended through great words? Explain how a word can heal a broken heart and a broken spirit.
8. Faith is great and easy to be restored. But how? Give three ways faith is restored.

9. Positive speech is the key to great confidence when applied. Explain the power of positive speech. Explain three types.
10. What is the power of confidence? Explain what it is and how it is. Why is it called the power of confidence?
11. I am afraid that some of us talk too much and others are stubborn with an attitude of "I can fix it my own self." Because of that attitude, it has destroyed many and brought families down to ruins. Explain why.
12. What is God to you and how? Explain.
13. What is the gold-on-silver picture?
14. What is the author of this book's motto?
15. What are the three principles concerning the power of mind?
16. Where do you see yourself twelve months from now in the Lord?

I put these questions in the book for you to answer. Answer for your learning.

1. What did Jehoshaphat do when he got word of the army encamped around them? List three things.
2. List the keys to our success.
3. Explain the nine areas that Satan has robbed from us.
4. Explain why the Seven We of Growth are so important.
5. Who are we in the Lord? Give eighteen answers.
6. List three ways that desperation can come in. List three ways to keep it from coming in.
7. If you understand your privilege, what do you understand? Explain. List three (must) to see God's word as it is.
8. List three of the greatest things Jehoshaphat did when in crisis. Can you apply what he did to your situation? Explain.
9. Is the power of positive thinking and positive speech a way of life? Explain how.
10. Pain comes in many forms and colors. But what do you do with the pain? When in distress, can you apply Psalm 55:22 to you, and can you receive it? Explain.
11. What helped Jehoshaphat keep his cool in the midst of this great test? List four ways to overcome and explain why it works.

12. Explain tribulation. What do you do in tribulation? Give at least three answers.
13. Can you overcome your problems? How?
14. How do we hear the voice of God, and where do we hear it?
15. How many ways does the voice of God come in? List.
16. What are the three (I), and what are the four (Him)? Name each of them and explain what it is to you.
17. List and explain five things that can affect your faith and how you feel about yourself.
18. What is the killer of the spirit and mind? List at least five.
19. Is desperation good for you? Explain both areas.
20. Define clarity in your life. List as many as you want to. Explain what clarity is to them. Explain it.
21. Can you look into the mirror and see where you need to start your healing? Let everyone look and explain what he sees.
22. Can you understand the term "comfort us in all our tribulation"? Who is comforted through your temptation? Explain how they are helped. Is temptation good for you?
23. Whose dirty laundry do you have? Explain. Do you have yours or someone else's?
24. How does this go with the prayer of desperation? What did Jehoshaphat do first in crisis? What did he do second? What did he do third?
25. List some pitfalls the devil has tried to throw at you.
26. Explain what the works of the flesh can destroy. List at least six.
27. Will desperation come to you? How? Explain how some desperation has come. Now explain what you did during the point of desperation.
28. Do you know that you know? Explain.
29. Can a battle be good for you? Explain.
30. What kingdom is there? List two types. What kingdom are we in? How did we get there?
31. Does what go in defile the temple? If so, explain.
32. Read the next paragraph and see if you know in whom you serve.

33. Explain some rotten apples you have covered up in your life. But beware of what you uncover.
34. Good words are what to you?
35. Describe an open rebuke. Explain why the need for true friends is so important. Describe how the conflict would have turned out if Jehoshaphat had panicked. Describe God's plan for this conflict for Jehoshaphat.
36. Words are a weapon against what situation? Explain.
37. How can this be when I am in the worst trial of my life?
38. Explain some of the pitfalls we can fall in if we are not on guard.
39. Explain the three factors that Jehoshaphat did. List each one and how you understand it. List what happened when Jehoshaphat called them together. Did Jehoshaphat have joy? How do you know?
40. What is your verdict on whether Paul could have joy in your tribulation or not? Could anyone?
41. What is desperation to you?
42. Why is patience after tribulation? Why is experience after patience? Why is hope after patience?
43. To have patience is to control one's action?
44. Which one of these traits is more important than the other? Answer all four of them separately.
45. What do you see makes you feel Jehoshaphat had the power of positive thinking and power of positive speech? Explain. There should be at least four answers.
46. Take a piece of paper and write the word *knowing* on each corner on the same side so you can see both words at the same time. Ask each one to look at it and answer it for themselves.
47. Are you unstable or stable? Ask it for yourself. Do you think Jehoshaphat was stable? Would you have done what he did?
48. List the four things Jehoshaphat did. List four things you would have done in the same circumstance.
49. In the title of this book, *Prayer of Desperation*, why was Jehoshaphat's prayer so important? What did he have that we may not have? What do we need to do to have more? It sums up in two words.

50. List some good seeds to grow on.
51. Why is it so important for us to live a sanctified life? Explain. Why did Jehoshaphat tell the people to cleanse their self? To walk with your mind in control is to walk in peace with God.
52. Can you change the way you think and speak? How do you change the way you think and speak? Answer it.
53. What are some of the provisions God has given unto us?
54. What does holding on to God's words mean? When you speak, I am somebody. What are you really saying?
55. What does receive it, to have it, mean to you?
56. What is faith? How did Jehoshaphat get his to trust God?
57. Explain what fearful and boldness mean to you.
58. What does it mean to get its attention when speaking to a mountain?
59. How do you cast seed upon the water? Can you receive your words spoken back unto you again?
60. Mays asked, "Are you what you speak?" Explain how that can be. Do your words reveal who you are? Think on that and answer. Explain the term *honeycomb* in Proverbs 16:24. Explain how the picture of silver and gold has related to some of your circumstances. Can you speak the word of a honeycomb to those who have just offended you? Can you put the gold of life upon the silver picture?
61. How is the word of faith increased in you? Explain two areas.
62. To find hidden treasure is to do what? List at least three areas in your life and in Jehoshaphat's life also.
63. Explain a good steward. Explain what loyalty is. Who should loyalty be to?
64. Why is it so important to always be honest and true with yourself? List some reasons why we are to think on positive things. List seven things we need to receive from the Lord.
65. To be just is to be what in Christ?
66. What does the pureness of oneself tell you about him?
67. Did Jehoshaphat have the spirit of a servant? If yes, explain.
68. What are virtue and praise together? Explain.

Chapter Sixteen

SCRIPTURE I USE IN PASSAGES FOR YOUR STUDY

- **2 Chronicles 20:1-4:** It came to pass after this also, that the children of Moab, and the children of Ammon, and with them other besides the Ammonites, came against Jehoshaphat to battle. Then there came some that told Jehoshaphat, saying. There cometh a great multitude against thee from beyond the sea on the side Syria, and behold, they be in Hazazontamar, which is Engedi. And Jehoshaphat feared, and set himself to seek the Lord, and proclaimed a fast throughout all Judah. And Judah gathered themselves together, to ask of the Lord: even out of all the cities of Judah came to seek the Lord.
- **John 4:29:** come see a man, which told me all things ever I did
- **Judges 2:10:** there rose another generation after them, which new not the Lord, nor yet the works which he had done for Israel.
- **Deuteronomy 29:2-6:** And all these blessing shall come on thee, and overtake thee, if thou shall hearken unto the voice of the Lord thy God. Blessed shall be the fruit of thy body, and the fruit of thy ground, and the fruit of thy cattle, the increase of thy kine, and the flock of thy sheep, Blessed shalt thou be when thou goest out. Blessed shall be thy basket and thy store. Blessed shalt thou be when thou comest in and blessed shalt thou be when

thou goest out. The Lord shall cause thine enemies that rise up against thee to be smitten before thy face; they shall come out against thee one way and flee before thee seven ways.

- **Deuteronomy 28:12–13:** ands thou lend too many nations, and thou shall not borrow. And the Lord shall make thee the head, and not the tail; and thou shall be above and not beneath.
- **3 John 2:** Beloved, I wish above all things that thou mayest prosper and be in health, even as thy.
- **Psalm 119:11:** Thy word have I hid in my heart, that I might not sin against thee.
- **Romans 4:17:** He calleth those things which be not as thou they were.

You need to start calling what you want.

- **Job 22:28:** Thou shall decree a thing, and it shall be established unto thee: and the light shall shine upon thy ways.
- **John 14:14:** And if ye shall ask any thing in my name, I will do it.
- **Matthew 16:18–19:** And I say unto thee, that thou art Peter, and upon this rock I will build my church; and the gates of hell shall not prevail against it. And I will give unto thee the keys of the kingdom of heaven: and whatsoever thou shall bind on earth shall be bound in heaven: and whatsoever thou shall loose on earth shall be loosed in heaven
- **Matthew 18:19:** Again I say unto you, That if two of you shall agree on earth as touching anything that they shall ask, it shall be done for them of my father which is in heaven.
- **Zechariah 4:6:** not by might, nor by power, but by my spirit saith the Lord of hosts.
- **John 4:24:** God is a spirit, and they that worship him must worship in spirit and in truth.
- **Romans 3:4:** God forbid: yea, let God be true, but every man a liar; as it is written.
- **2 Chronicles 20:7:** Art thou not our God, who didst drive out the inhabitants of this land before thy people Israel, and gavest it to the seed of Abraham thy friend for ever.

- **2 Chronicle 17:8–9:** and with them he sent Levites, even Shem-a-i-ah, and Neth-a-niah, and Zeb-a-di-ah, and Asa-hel, and She-mir-a-moth, and Je-hona-than, and Ad-o-ni-jah, and To-bi-ah,Tob-ad-onijah,Levites: and with them Elish-a-ma and Jehoram priest. And they taught in Judah and had the book of the law with them, and went about throughout all the cities of Judah and taught the people.
- **2 Chronicle 20:1:** It came to pass after this also, that the children of Moab, and the children of Ammon, and with them other beside the Ammonites, came against Jehoshaphat to battle.
- **Lamentations 3:21:** This I recall to my mind, therefore have I hope.
- **2 Chronicles 20:3:** And Jehoshaphat feared, and set himself to seek the Lord, and proclaimed a fast throughout all Judah.
- **Matthew 17:21:** this kind goeth not out but by prayer and fasting.
- **2 Chronicles 20:5–6:** And Jehoshaphat stood in the congregation of Judah and Jerusalem, in the house of the Lord, and before the court. And said Lord God of our father, are not thou God in heaven? And rulest not thou over all the kingdom of our heathen? And in thy hand is there not power and might, so that none is able to withstand thee?
- **Matthew 7:7–8:** Ask, and it shall be given you; seek, and ye shall find; knock, and it shall be opened unto you: For everyone that asketh receiveth; and he that seeketh findeth; and to him that knocketh it shall be opened.
- **Matthew 10:29–31:** Are not sparrow sold for a farthing? and one of them shall not fall on the ground without your father. But the very hairs of your head are all numbered. Fear ye not therefore, ye are more value than many sparrows.
- **Psalm 55:22:** Cast thy burdens upon the Lord, and he shall sustain thee: he shall never suffer the righteous to be moved.
- **Isaiah 5:8:** For my thoughts are not your thought, neither are your ways my ways, saith the Lord.
- **2 Corinthians 1:4:** Who comforteth us in all our tribulation, that we may be able to comfort them which are in any trouble, by the comfort wherewith we ourselves are comforted of God.

- **Matthew 10:8:** Heal the sick, cleanse the lepers, raise the dead, cast out devils: freely ye have received freely give.
- **Isaiah 55:6:** Seek ye the Lord while he may be found, call upon him while he is near.
- **Habakkuk 2:1:** I will stand upon my watch, and set me upon the tower, and will watch to see what he will say unto me, and I shall answer when I am reproved.
- **1 Samuel 15:22:** Behold, to obey is better than sacrifice.
- **Psalm 91:15:** He shall call upon me and I will answer him: I will be with him in trouble; I will deliver him, and honor him.
- **James 5:16:** Confess your faults one to another, and pray one for another, that he may be healed.
- **Corinthians 10:13:** There hath no temptation taken you but such as is common to man: but God is faithful, who will not suffer you to be tempted above that ye are able; but with the temptation also make away to escape, that ye may be able to bear it.
- **Corinthians 1:4:** Who comforteth us in all our tribulation, that we may be able to comfort them which are in any trouble, by the comfort wherewith we ourselves are comforted of God.
- **Proverbs 16:18:** Pride goeth before destruction, and a haughty spirit before a fall.
- **Romans 14:7:** For none of us liveth to himself and no man dieth to himself.
- **Genesis 4:9:** And the Lord said unto Cain, where is Able thy brother? And he said I know not: Am I my brother keeper.
- **Galatians 6:1:** Brethren, if a man be overtaken in a fault, ye which are spiritual, restore such an one in the spirit meekness; considering thyself, lest thou also be tempted.
- **Galatians 5:21–22:** But the fruit if the spirits is love, joy, peace, longsuffering, gentleness, goodness, faith, meekness, temperance against such there is no law.
- **John 15:15:** For I call you not servants; for the servant knoweth not what his Lord doeth; but I have called you friends.
- **Matthew 10:28:** And fear not them which kill the body but are not able to kill the soul: but rather fear him which is able to destroy both soul and body in hell.

- **John 10:10:** The thief cometh not, but for to seal, and to kill, and to destroy.
- **2 Chronicles 20:12–13:** O our God, wilt thou not judge them? For we have no might against this great company that cometh against us; neither know we what to do: but our eyes are upon thee. And all Judah stood before the Lord, with their little ones, their wives, and their children.
- **2 Chronicles 20:14–15:** Then upon Jahaziel the son of Zechariah, the son of Benaiah, the son of Jeiel, the son of Mattaniah, a Levite of the son of Asaph, came the spirit if the Lord un the mist of the congregation; And ye said, Hearken ye, all Judah, and the inhabitants of Jerusalem, and thou King Jehoshaphat, Thus said the Lord unto you, Be not afraid nor dismayed by reason of this great multitude, for the battle is not yours, but God's.
- **Exodus 33:20:** And he said, thou canst not see my face: for there shall no man see me, and live.
- **Exodus 33:19:** And he said, I will make all my goodness pass before thee.
- **James 1:13–14:** Let no man say when he is tempted, I am tempted of God: for God cannot be tempted with evil, neither tempted he any man: But every man is tempted when he draws away of his own lust and enticed.
- **Colossians 1:13:** Who hath delivered us out n of the power of darkness, and hath translated us into the kingdom of his dear son: In who, we have redemption thought his blood, even the forgiveness of sins.
- **Luke 6:45:** for of the abundance of the heart his mouth speaketh.
- **Exodus 14:13:** Fear does not stand still and see the salvation of the Lord.
- **Proverbs 12:25:** Heaviness in the heart of man maketh it stoops but a good word maketh it glad.
- **Ecclesiastes 7:5:** It is better to hear the rebuke of the wise, than for a man to hear the song of fools.
- **Romans 10:17:** So then faith cometh by hearing, and hearing by the word of the Lord

- **James 1:22:** But be ye doers of the word, and not hearers only, deceiving your own selves.
- **Luke 17:5:** And the Apostles said unto the Lord, increase our faith.
- **Mark 11:23:** For verily I say unto you, that whosoever shall say unto this mountain, be thou removed, and be thou cast into the sea; and shall not doubt in his heart, but shall believe that those things which he saith shall come to pass, he shall have whatsoever he saith.
- **1 Peter 1:8:** Whom having not seen, ye love, in whom, through now ye see him not, yet believing, ye rejoice with joy unspeakable and full of glory.
- **James 1:2:** Brethren count it all joy when ye fall into divers' temptation.
- **John 15:11:** These things have I spoke unto you, that my joy may be in you, and that your joy may be made full.
- **Nehemiah 10:8:** the joy of the Lord, in your strength.
- **2 Corinthians 7:4:** Great is my boldness of speech toward you, great is my glorying of you: I am filled with comfort, I am exceeding joyful in all our tribulation.
- **Matthew 5:44:** But I say unto you, Love your enemies, bless them that curse you, do good to them that hate you, and pray for them which despitefully use you, and persecute you.
- **John 15:20:** Remember the words that I said unto you, the servant is not greater than his Lord. If they persecute me they will also persecute you; if they have kept my saying, they will keep your also:
- **Romans 5:1–4:** Therefore being justified by faith, we have peace with God through our Lord Jesus Christ: By whom also we have access by faith into this grace wherein we stand and rejoice in hope of the glory of God. And not only so, but we glory in tribulation also: knowing that tribulation worketh patience; and patience, experience, and experience hope: And hope maketh not ashamed; because the love of God is shed abroad in our hearts by the Holy Ghost which is given unto us.

- **James 1:4:** to let patience have her perfect work, that ye may be perfect and entire, wanting nothing.
- **Matthew 6:33:** But seek ye first the kingdom of God, and his righteousness; and all these things shall be added unto you.
- **James 1:8:** A double minded man is unstable in all his ways.
- **Philippians 4:8:** Finally, brethren, whatsoever things are true, whatsoever things are honest, whatsoever things are just, whatsoever things are pure, whatsoever things are lovely, whatsoever things are of good report; if there be any virtue, and there be any praise, think on these things.
- **2 Corinthians 1:4:** Who comforteth us in all our tribulation, that we may be able to comfort them which are in any trouble, by the comfort wherewith we ourselves are comforted of God.
- **Song of Solomon 2:15:** Take us the foxes, the little foxes that spoil the vines: for our vines have tender grapes.
- **Luke 6:45:** A good man out of the good treasure of his heart bringeth forth that which is good; and an evil man out of the evil treasure of his heart bringeth forth that which in evil: for of the abundance of the heart his mouth speaketh.
- **John 17:17:** Sanctify them through thy truth; thy word is truth.
- **Philippians 1:12:** work out our own salvation with fear and trembling.
- **Isaiah 35:8:** And an highway shall be there, and a way, and it shall be called "The way of holiness;" the unclean shall not pass over it; but it shall be for those; the wayfaring men, through fools, shall not "err" therein.
- **Luke 9:23:** if any man will come after me, let him deny himself, and take up his cross daily, and follow me.
- **Proverbs 22:28:** Remove not the ancient landmark, which thy fathers have set).
- **Hebrews 4:16:** Lets us therefore come boldly unto the throne of grace, that we may obtain mercy, and find help in the time of need.
- **Philippians 4:6:** Be careful for nothing; but in everything by prayer and supplication with thanksgiving let your request be made know unto God.

- **Numbers 35:6:** And among the cities which ye shall give unto the Levites there shall be six cities for refuge, which ye shall appoint for the manslayer that he may flee thither.
- **Numbers 35:15:** These six cities shall be a refuge, both for the children of Israel, and for the sojourner among them; that every one that kill any person unaware may flee thither.
- **Job 1:1:** There was a man in the land of Uz, whose name was Job; and that man was perfect and upright, and one that feared God, and eschewed evil.
- **Revelation 3:20:** Behold I stand at the door and knock: if any hear my voice, and open the door, I will come into him, and will sup with him, and he with me.
- **Acts 10:34:** Then Peter opens his mouth, and said, of a truth I perceive that God is no respecter of person.
- **John 1:1:** In the beginning was the word, and the word was with God, and the word was God.
- **Psalm 55:22:** Cast thy burdens upon the Lord, and he shall sustain thee, he shall never suffer the righteous to be move.
- **Mark 11:23:** For verily I say unto you, that whosoever shall say unto this mountain, be thou removed, and be thou cast into the sea; and shall not doubt in his heart but shall believe that those things which he saith shall come to pass, he shall have whatsoever he saith.
- **Psalm 1:1–3:** Blessed is the man that walketh not in the counsel of the ungodly, nor standeth in the way of sinner, nor sitteth in the seat of the scornful. But his delight is in the law of the Lord; and his law doth he meditate day and night. And he shall be like a tree planted by the rivers of water, that bringeth forth his fruit in his season; his leaf shall not with; and whatsoever he doeth shall prosper.
- **Romans 10:17:** So then faith cometh by hearing, and hearing by the word of God.
- **2 Chronicles 20:7:** Art not thou our God, who didst drive out the inhabitants of this land before thy people Israel.
- **Ecclesiastes 11:1:** Cast thy bread upon the water: for thou shall find it after many days.

- **Proverbs 18:21:** Death and life are in the power of the tongue: and they that love it shall eat the fruit thereof.
- **Matthew 7:12:** Judge not, that ye be not judged. For with what judgment ye judge, ye shall be judged: and with what measure ye mete, it shall be measure to you again.
- **James 1:10:** Out of the same mouth proceedeth blessing and cursing. My brethren, these things ought not so to be.
- **2 Corinthians 9:10:** Now he that ministered seed to the sower both minister bread for your food, and multiply your seed sown, and increase the fruits of your righteousness.
- **Matthew 7:12:** Judge not, that ye be not judged. For with what judgment ye judge, ye shall be judged: and with what measure ye mete, it shall be measure to you again.
- **Proverbs 16:24:** Pleasant words are as a honeycomb, sweet to the soul, and health to the bones.
- **Proverbs 25:11:** A word fitly spoken is like apples of gold in picture of silver.
- **Romans 10:17:** So then faith cometh by hearing and hearing by the word of God.
- **1 John 2:27:** But the anointing which ye receive of him abideth in you, and ye need not that any man teach you, but as the same anointing teacheth you of all things, and is no lie, even as it hath taught you, ye shall abide in him.
- **Isaiah 45:3:** I will give thee hidden riches of secret places.
- **3 John 2:** Beloved, I wish above all thing that thou mayest prosper and be in health even as thy soul prospered.
- **Psalm 91:15:** He called upon me and I will answer him: I will be with him in trouble: I will deliver him, and honor him.
- **Ecclesiastes 2:11:** Then I look on all my works that my hands had wrought, and on the labor that I labor. To do: and behold, all was vanity and vexation of the spirit, and there wan no profit under the sun.
- **2 Corinthians 10:4–5:** For the weapons of our warfare are not carnal, but mightily through God to the pulling down of strong holds.

- **Proverbs 16:24:** Pleasant words are as an honeycomb, sweet to the soul, and health to the bones.
- **James 2:19:** The devils also believed and tremble.
- **Proverbs 10:12:** Hatred stirreth up strifes: But love covereth all sins.
- **James 5:20:** Let him know, that he which converteth the sinner from his way shall save a soul from death and hide a multitude of sins.
- **Acts 10:22:** And they said, Cornelius the centurion, a (JUST) man, and one that feareth God.
- **Matthew 1:19:** Then Joseph her husband, being a (JUST) man, and not willing to make her publick example, was minded to put her away privily.
- **Proverbs 24:16:** For a (JUST) man falleth seven times, and riseth up again: but the wicked shall fall into mischief.
- **Matthew 7:1-2:** Judge not, that ye be not judge. For with what judgment ye judge, and with what measure ye mete, it shall be measure to you again.
- **Ephesians 6:12:** For we wrestle not against flesh and blood, but, against principalities, against powers, against the rulers of darkness of this world, against spiritual wickedness in high places.
- **John 10:10:** The thief cometh not, but for to steal, and to kill, and to destroy I am come that might they have life and that they might have it more abundantly.
- **Matthew 16:19:** And I will give unto you thee keys of the kingdom of heaven: and whatsoever thou shalt bind on earth shall be bound in heaven: and whatsoever thou shalt loose on earth shalt be loosed in heaven.
- **Isaiah 5:11:** So shall my word be that goeth forth out of my mouth: it shall not return unto me void, but it shall accomplish that which I please, and it shall prosper in the thing whereto I sent it.
- **Matthew 23:12:** And whosoever shall exalt himself shall be abased; and he that shall humble himself shall be exalted.

Printed in the United States
by Baker & Taylor Publisher Services